SOUNDINGS

SOUNDINGS

Robert A. Raines

HARPER & ROW, PUBLISHERS

NEW YORK, EVANSTON, AND LONDON

For Bobby

LIBRARY OF CONGRESS CATALOG CARD NUMBER: 73-85066

Acknowledgment is made to the following for permission to reprint copyrighted material:

AKRON BEACON JOURNAL for portions of a letter printed in the *Akron Beacon Journal*, March 27, 1967.

SVETLANA ALLILUYEVA for extract from her article, "To Boris Leonidovich Pasternak," copyright © 1967 by Copex Establishment.

AMERICAN BIBLE SOCIETY for verses from *Today's English Version of the New Testament*, copyright © 1966 by the American Bible Society.

ATHENEUM PUBLISHERS, INC., for extract from *African Genesis* by Robert Ardrey, copyright © 1961 by Literat S.A.; extract from *The Captain* by Jan de Hartog, copyright © 1966 by Littra A.G.

AVON BOOKS for extract from *The Me Nobody Knows* by Stephen M. Joseph, copyright © 1969 by Stephen M. Joseph.

RICHARD W. BARON PUBLISHING COMPANY, INC., for extract from "Intimations of Mortality" (*United Church Herald*, August 1968) and "Gift from a Hairdryer" (*United Church Herald*, November 1962) by Mary Jean Irion, appearing in her book *Yes, World: A Mosaic of Meditation*, copyright © 1970 by Mary Jean Irion.

CAMBRIDGE UNIVERSITY PRESS for verses from *The New English Bible, New Testament*, © 1961 by The Delegates of the Oxford University Press and The Syndics of the Cambridge University Press.

DOUBLEDAY & COMPANY, INC., for verses from *The Jerusalem Bible*, copyright © 1966 by Darton, Longman & Todd Ltd. and Doubleday & Co., Inc.

E. P. DUTTON & CO., INC., for extract from the book *nigger:* AN AUTOBIOGRAPHY by Dick Gregory with Robert Lipsyte, copyright © 1964 by Dick Gregory Enterprises, Inc.

GROSSET & DUNLAP, INC., for extract from *A Death in the Family* by James Agee, copyright © 1957 by The James Agee Trust.

HARPER & ROW, PUBLISHERS, INC., for extract from *More than Meets the Eye* by Carl Mydans, copyright © 1959 by Carl Mydans; extract from *The First Circle* by Aleksandr I. Solzhenitsyn, Translated from the Russian by Thomas P. Whitney, copyright © 1968 by Harper & Row, Publishers, Inc.

ALFRED A. KNOPF, INC., copyright © 1964 by John Updike, for extract reprinted from *The Music School* by John Updike. First appeared in *The New Yorker*.

LOOK MAGAZINE Editors for extract from "It's OK to Cry in the Office" by John Poppy, August 9, 1968, copyright © 1969 by Cowles Communications, Inc.

Contents

Preface

I wish to express my appreciation to the many people who have helped and encouraged the writing of this book. Ideas for the selections have come from many sources. Lillie Fraser typed the material with her characteristic competence and grace. Joan Hemenway has provided invaluable assistance in the selection of material, Biblical passages, and editing of the entire manuscript. The book is considerably better than it might have been without her creative scrutiny. My family has once again been willing to let me work while on our vacation. Finally I am grateful to the Biblical heritage for its wide and deep humanity, and to the marvelous human beings whose stories appear in this book, whose courage, anguish, and hope have moved me, and I hope will also move you, to become a more truly human being according to the deepest wisdom of your own religious tradition or quest.

Introduction

Aleksandr Solzhenitsyn, in his novel *The First Circle*, writes:

In every human being's life there is one period when he manifests himself most fully, feels most profoundly himself, and acts with the deepest effect on himself and others. And whatever happens to that person from that time on, no matter how outwardly significant, it is all a letdown. We remember, get drunk on, play over and over in many different keys, sing over and over to ourselves that snatch of a song that sounded just once within us. For some, that period comes in childhood, and they stay children all their lives. For others it comes with first love, and these are the people who spread the myth that love comes only once. Those for whom it was the period of their greatest wealth, honor, or power will still in old age be mumbling with toothless gums of their lost grandeur. For Nerzhin, prison was such a time. For Shchagov, it was the war.

For you, what was the time when that snatch of a song sounded within, when you were most deeply in touch with your own humanity?

Does that song sound only once?

Or does it sound again and again after you have first heard it resonating within, often faintly in memory or hope, but sometimes throbbing in loud echoes here and now?

The purpose of *Soundings* is to intrigue us to listen for that strange yet familiar song of humanity, to recognize and hearken to it when and wherever we hear it.

The hope of *Soundings* is to enable us to experience our own humanity more profoundly, and to act with the deepest effect on others.

Soundings is a grand canyon of humanity in song. It is an exploration of depth-takings in our private and public lives. It is a venture of responding to the echoes resonating from

11

the heart of a fearful child, a husband pondering his infidelity, a young soldier learning what the spirit of the bayonet is, a teen-age girl leaving home because her parents can't listen to her, a businessman in confrontation with his colleagues, a young man on the make making it, young and old experiencing grief, death, courage, joy.

The thirty-four selections have one thing in common—each of them sounded that song of humanity in me. I hope they will do the same for you. They come from playwrights and prisoners, novelists and newsmen, parents and children, anthropologists and analysts of the stock market, the very rich and the very poor, sportsmen and businessmen, ordinary and extraordinary people. There are Jews here, and Catholics, Protestants, Hindus, Buddhists, Moslems, agnostics, and atheists. You and I are hiding in each selection waiting to hear and be heard. Some selections will awaken a long-forgotten episode in your own life with all its meanings; some will trigger exciting new possibilities for awareness and action.

Matched with the selections are Biblical passages or episodes which sound a similar song. We find ourselves hearing a modern and an ancient testimony to the same human experience across the ages and in the depths of each human being. A dialogue begins. We discover that the people of the Bible are as wonderfully-terribly human as any modern company of people. These Biblical people free us from the tyranny of the present by providing an ancient backdrop against which to perceive and hear the contemporary drama of our own lives and times. The ancient and modern witnesses illuminate and confront one another, and you and I are in the middle of it, listening. More often than getting an answer to a question, we will find our own questions raised in fresh, compelling ways. There will come the shock of recognition, and the sound of a strange yet familiar song.

Completing each unit are reflections, which are my own responses to the ancient-modern dialogue. So you and I will be in conversation too. Sometimes your thoughts will wing off

12

in an entirely different direction from my own. When that happens swing away, and maybe even jot down your own comment, poem, prayer, or random insight. Some of your own soundings may be valuable insights which you will want to record and remember. Other times you and I will be tuning in on the same wave length. When that happens let's sing that old-new song together! Above all, plumb the depths of these readings, and be enriched and encouraged.

Hello Human Being!

Morris Dalmatofsky, known for more than three decades to the habitués of Times Square as "the walking department store," died Friday in his one-room apartment at 357 West 29th Street. His age was 65.

To the police and the store owners, he was Morris the Peddler, a man who brought with him an assortment of toothpaste, razor blades, candy, socks and other small items that he sold in luncheonettes or other shops, his only offices.

All year Mr. Dalmatofsky visited the Times Square area. All year he wore the dark cap and vest that came to be identified with him.

As he moved about he passed out royal titles to those he met. There were "King Jack," "Queen Sadie" and "Count Mike." If there was no title, his greeting was a simple, "Hello human being."

Mr. Dalmatofsky told little about himself and yet told much of what he was. His answers to questions on this subject were evasive. "Woe is me," he would say; or "Why was I born?"; or "I'm an unfortunate human being." Those comments only brought him a wider following.

Friends in Times Square said he had only one fetish, thorough honesty. He would not overcharge for an item he sold; he would not keep the change; he would not take anything he could not pay for.

In his room, there was evidence he was a prolific reader. Magazines dating back more than 10 years were still open to pages where he had not finished stories. There was also a collection of books he had read.

A funeral service will be held today at 2 P.M. at Gutterman's Chapel, 1970 Broadway.   —NEW YORK TIMES

15

He entered Jericho and was going through the town when a man whose name was Zaccheus made his appearance; he was one of the senior tax collectors and a wealthy man. He was anxious to see what kind of man Jesus was, but he was too short and could not see him for the crowd; so he ran ahead and climbed a sycamore tree to catch a glimpse of Jesus who was to pass that way. When Jesus reached the spot he looked up and spoke to him: "Zaccheus, come down. Hurry, because I must stay at your house today." And he hurried down and welcomed him joyfully. They all complained when they saw what was happening. "He has gone to stay at a sinner's house," they said. But Zaccheus stood his ground and said to the Lord, "Look, sir, I am going to give half my property to the poor, and if I have cheated anybody I will pay him back four times the amount." And Jesus said to him, "Today salvation has come to this house, because this man too is a son of Abraham; for the Son of Man has come to seek out and save what was lost."

—LUKE 19:1–10 (JB)

I look up at your heavens, made by your fingers,
at the moon and stars you set in place.
Ah, what is man that you should spare a thought for him,
the son of man that you should care for him?

Yet you have made him little less than a god,
you have crowned him with glory and splendour,
made him Lord over the work of your hands,
set all things under his feet.

—PSALM 8:3–6 (JB)

Hello human being!

Hello	Zacchaeus	Goodby	scoundrel
	John		boss
	George		subordinate

Hello	black man	Goodby	militant
	white man		racist
	black power		black weakness
	white power		white privilege

Hello	cop	Goodby	pig
	kid		delinquent
	man		computer
	woman		sex machine

Hello	Jew	Goodby	kike
	Catholic		papist
	Protestant		separated brother

Hello	soldier	Goodby	General Hershey
	F.B.I.		Mr. Hoover

Hello	Jesus	Goodby	Superman
	Paul		Pope

Hello	Dad	Goodby	father figure
	Mom		Portnoy's mother

Hello	you	Goodby	enemy
	me		#1

Hello human being!

I'm Proud of Myself

I first knew Michael as a wan little boy who needed a sturdy wood wheel chair to help him sit up. His black eyes punctuated a blue white face over which riffled just a whisper of a smile when he was wheeled into the craft shop. In those days he could not sit up unsupported, or talk, or use his hands or legs for anything but uncoordinated motions.

A summer passed and the next time I saw Michael he was full of bounce. Bright eyed and rosy cheeked, he pushed himself up and down in his chair shouting for joy. It was still pretty difficult to do more than hold a paint brush and daub, or to pound and push the clay.

And then months and another year passed and here was Michael promoted from a special class for severely handicapped youngsters to third grade! Those hands still didn't behave very well but he had made them write what he is not able to say quite clearly enough as yet. With unbelieving hope we started to weave on a simple frame with loopers. Day by day we struggled with the loops flying off the table and slipping off the pegs of the frame, but it became clear that this weaving was going to be a potholder. Michael comes in now singing and pushing his chair, which he only needs when he walks all the way down the corridor. When he sits down to work he must first admire his beautiful weaving and hug it close because there is not a single mistake, and this will be a gift to take home.

The other day was Michael's eleventh birthday, so the other children said. We congratulated him and told him how happy we were that he was doing so well, and even getting around to put his own tools away now. He tried to tell me something I couldn't quite understand, but he said he could write it. And here it is in all its joyful dignity of the child—a gift to share . . .

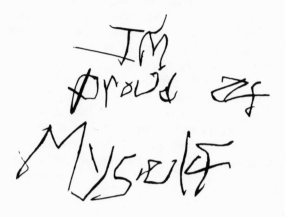

I'M proud of Myself

—GRACE CRAWFORD

And the people of Israel groaned under their bondage, and cried out for help, and their cry under bondage came up to God. And God heard their groaning, and God remembered his covenant with Abraham, with Isaac, and with Jacob. And God saw the people of Israel, and God knew their condition.
—EXODUS 2:23–25 (RSV)

When he returned to Capernaum some time later, word went around that he was back; and so many people collected that there was no room left, even in front of the door. He was preaching the word to them when some people came bringing him a paralytic carried by four men, but as the crowd made it impossible to get the man to him, they stripped the roof over the place where Jesus was; and when they had made an opening, they lowered the stretcher on which the paralytic lay. Seeing their faith, Jesus said to the paralytic, "My child, your sins are forgiven." Now some scribes were sitting there, and they thought to themselves, "How can this man talk like that? He is blaspheming. Who can forgive sins but God?" Jesus, inwardly aware that this was what they were thinking, said to them, "Why do you have these thoughts in your hearts? Which of these is easier: to say to the paralytic, 'Your sins are forgiven' or to say, 'Get up, pick up your stretcher and walk'? But to prove to you that the Son of Man has authority on earth to forgive sins,"—he said to the paralytic—"I order you: get up, pick up your stretcher, and go off home." And the man got up, picked up his stretcher at once and walked out in front of every one, so that they were all astounded and praised God saying, 'We have never seen anything like this."

—MARK 2:1–11 (JB)

Today it's hard for me
to be proud of myself
and to have the joyful dignity
of a child
because I'm ashamed of myself
today
and think I'm no damn good
to any one

It's like being buried
in myself
and I can't get out
alive

I need help
I need friends
who will believe in me
with unbelieving hope
Give me such friends
now
and make me such a friend

Do You believe in me
even when
I don't believe in me . . .
or You?
Tell me
to get up out of my self-pity
and walk!
Teach me
to weave my life
without so many mistakes
Try me
and
I'll try.
Okay?

Someone's Crying, Lord

> *What you do*
> > *to one of the least of these*
> > > *my brothers*
> > *you*
> > > *do*
> > > > *to*
> > > > > *me*

Dear Mom and Dad:

Today we went on a mission and I'm not very proud of myself, my friends or my country. We burned every hut in sight!

It was a small rural network of villages and the people were incredibly poor. My unit burned and plundered their meager possessions. Let me try to explain the situation to you.

The huts here are thatched palm leaves. Each one has a dried mud bunker inside. These bunkers are to protect the families. Kind of like air raid shelters.

My unit commanders, however, chose to think that these bunkers are offensive. So every hut we find that has a bunker, we are ordered to burn to the ground!

When the 10 helicopters landed this morning, in the midst of these huts, and six men jumped out of each "chopper" we were firing the moment we hit the ground. We fired into all the huts we could. Then we got "on line" and swept the area.

It is then that we burn these huts and take all men old enough to carry a weapon and the "choppers" come and get them (they take them to a collection point a few miles away for interrogation). The families don't understand this. The Viet Cong fill their minds with tales saying the GIs kill all their men.

So, everyone is crying, begging and praying that we don't separate them and take their husbands and fathers, sons and grandfathers. The women wail and moan.

Then they watch in terror as we burn their homes, personal possessions and food. Yes, we burn all rice and shoot all livestock.

Some of the guys are so careless! Today a buddy of mine called "La Dai" ("Come here") into a hut and an old man came out of the bomb shelter. My buddy told the old man to get away from the hut and since we have to move quickly on a sweep, just threw a hand grenade into the shelter.

As he pulled the pin the old man got excited and started jabbering and running toward my buddy and the hut. A GI, not understanding, stopped the old man with a football tackle just as my buddy threw the grenade into the shelter. (There is a four-second delay on a hand grenade.)

After he threw it, and was running for cover, (during this four-second delay) we all heard a baby crying from inside the shelter!

There was nothing we could do . . .

After the explosion we found the mother, two children (ages about 6 and 12, boy and girl) and an almost newborn baby. That is what the old man was trying to tell us!

The shelter was small and narrow. They were all huddled together. The three of us dragged out the bodies onto the floor of the hut.

IT WAS HORRIBLE!!

The children's fragile bodies were torn apart, literally mutilated. We looked at each other and burned the hut.

The old man was just whimpering in disbelief outside the burning hut. We walked away and left him there.

My last look was: an old, old man in ragged, torn, dirty clothes on his knees outside the burning hut, praying to Buddha. His white hair was blowing in the wind and tears were rolling down. . . .

YOUR SON

—Portions of a letter printed in the Akron Beacon Journal, March 27, 1967

And Absalom chanced to meet the servants of David. Absalom was riding upon his mule, and the mule went under the thick branches of a great oak, and his head caught fast in the oak, and he was left hanging between heaven and earth, while the mule that was under him went on. . . .

Now David was sitting between the two gates; and the watchman went up to the roof of the gate by the wall, and when he lifted up his eyes and looked, he saw a man running alone. And the watchman called out and told the king. And the king said, "If he is alone, there are tidings in his mouth." And he came apace and drew near. . . .

And behold, the Cushite came; and the Cushite said, "Good tidings for my lord the king! For the Lord has delivered you this day from the power of all who rose up against you." The king said to the Cushite, "Is it well with the young man Absalom?" And the Cushite answered, "May the enemies of my lord the king, and all who rise up against you for evil, be like that young man." And the king was deeply moved, and went up to the chamber over the gate, and wept; and as he went, he said, "O my son Absalom, my son, my son Absalom! Would I had died instead of you, O Absalom, my son, my son!"

—2 SAMUEL 18:9, 24–25, 31–33 (RSV)

And when he drew near and saw the city he wept over it, saying, "Would that even today you knew the things that make for peace! But now they are hid from your eyes. For the days shall come upon you, when your enemies will cast up a bank about you and surround you, and hem you in on every side, and dash you to the ground, you and your children within you, and they will not leave one stone upon another in you; because you did not know the time of your visitation."

—LUKE 19:41–44 (RSV)

It's April 4 today
Two years ago a man was murdered
in Memphis
He died to save us
from hate
and cruelty

How careless is my cruelty
to innocent people
in Vietnam
the ghetto
the office
the family room

It's April 4 today
Two thousand years ago
a man was murdered
in Jerusalem
He died to save us
from hate
and cruelty

How many ears must one man have
before
he can hear people
cry?

Someone's crying, Lord

A Young Stud

Folsom Prison,
October 28, 1965

Once I was walking down Main Street in L. A. around noon on a Saturday and it was a beautiful sunny day. I was just a young stud about sixteen, I guess, and I had one of those I-think-I'm-cute-type walks, prancing and rolling on my toes. Before me and adjacent to the sidewalk was a shoeshine stand facing in my direction. A jukebox was blaring a tune of the times and I got caught up in the music as I walked along. I was kind of walking in time to the music. Sitting up on the customer's seat was a big fine sister who was popping her fingers and wiggling to the music and smiling at me because our eyes had met. There was no one else in the shinestand and just as I came up even with the stand the record ended and I stopped in my tracks, staring at the girl in a fascinated stupor. Then, without warning, she sang: "Beautiful, beautiful brown eyes." Wow. That did me in, cleaned me out, and I realized that I was standing there gaping at her like a country fool. I was really confused and embarrassed and I cut out, completely blowing my cool. And as I split, I saw her cracking up with kicks.

—ELDRIDGE CLEAVER

I am black but lovely, daughters of Jerusalem,
like the tents of Kedar,
like the pavilions of Salmah. . . .

I hear my Beloved.
See how he comes.

leaping on the mountains,
bounding over the hills.
My Beloved is like a gazelle,
like a young stag.

See where he stands
behind our wall.
He looks in at the window,
he peers through the lattice.

My Beloved lifts up his voice,
he says to me, . .
"Come then, my love,
my lovely one, come.
For see, winter is past,
the rains are over and gone.
The flowers appear on the earth.
The season of glad songs has come,
the cooing of the turtledove is heard in our land.
The fig tree is forming its first figs
and the blossoming vines give out their fragrance.
Come then, my love,
my lovely one, come.
My dove, hiding in the clefts of the rock,
in the coverts of the cliff,
show me your face,
let me hear your voice;
for your voice is sweet
and your face is beautiful."
—SONG OF SONGS 1:5, 2:8—14 (JB)

Oh!
the power of her beauty
Oh!
the shock of her boldness
Oh!
the thrill of her desire

Go young lovers and
make love
welcome
Laugh and live and
love while it is forever
wiggle and wink
clap your hands
snap your fingers
   and sing, oh
    sing the spring!

Taste spring
drink its wine
smell spring
breathe its fragrance
touch spring
embrace its beauty
dance spring
bounce its beat
and swing on down
the avenue
   laughing
      oh laughing!

I'm Sorry

Murray, the jobless rebel against square society, has gone out to try to get a job for the sake of Sandra, the square social worker who came to save him and winds up loving him. He comes back and tells her what happened.

MURRAY: (Takes her arm, smiles, seats her on the chair in front of him) I shall now leave you breathless with the strange and wondrous tale of this sturdy lad's adventures today in downtown Oz.—Picture me, if you will, me. I am walking on East Fifty-first Street an hour ago and I decided to construct and develop a really decorative, general-*all-purpose apology*. No complicated, just the words "I am sorry," said with a little style.

SANDRA: Sorry for what?

MURRAY: Anything. For being late, early, stupid, asleep, silly, alive. Well, you know, when you're walking down the street talking to yourself how sometimes you suddenly say a couple words out loud? So I said, "I'm sorry," and this fella, complete stranger, he looks up a second and says, "That's all right, Mac," and goes right on. (Murray and Sandra laugh) He automatically forgave me. I communicated. Five o'clock rush-hour in midtown you could say, "Sir, I believe your hair is on fire," and they wouldn't hear you. So I decided to test the whole thing out scientifically. I stayed right there on the corner of Fifty-first and Lex for a while, just saying "I'm sorry" to everybody that went by. (abjectly) "Oh, I'm so sorry, sir . . ." (slowly, quaveringly) "I'm terribly sorry, madam . . ." (warmly) "Say there, miss, I'm sorry." Of course, some people just gave me a funny look, but, Sandy, I swear, seventy-five percent of them *for-*

gave me. (acting out the people for her) "Forget it, buddy" . . . "That's O.K., really." Two ladies forgave me in unison, one fella forgave me from a passing car, and one guy forgave me for his dog, "Poofer forgives the nice man, don't you, Poofer?" Oh, Sandy, it was fabulous. I had tapped some vast reservoir. Something had happened to all of them for which they felt *some*body should apologize. If you went up to people on the street and offered them money, they'd refuse it. But everybody accepts apology immediately. It is the most negotiable currency. I said to them, "I am sorry." And they were all so generous, so kind. You could give 'em love and it wouldn't be accepted half as graciously, as unquestioningly . . .

SANDRA: (after a pause) Murray, you didn't take any of the jobs.

MURRAY: (quietly) Sandy, I took whatever I am and put a suit on it and gave it a haircut and took it outside and that's what happened. I know what I said this morning, what I promised, and Sandra, I'm sorry. I'm very sorry. —HERB GARDNER

If your brother does something wrong, reprove him and, if he is sorry, forgive him. And if he wrongs you seven times a day and seven times comes back to you and says, "I am sorry," you must forgive him. —LUKE 17:4 (JB)

And so the kingdom of heaven may be compared to a king who decided to settle his accounts with his servants. When the reckoning began, they brought him a man who owed ten thousand talents, but he had no means of paying, so his master gave orders that he should be sold, together with his wife and children and all his possessions, to meet the debt. At this, the servant threw himself down at his master's feet. "Give me time," he said, "and I will pay the whole sum." And the servant's master felt so sorry for him that he let him go and cancelled the debt. Now as this servant went out, he happened to meet a fellow servant who owed him one hundred denarii, and he seized him by the throat and began to throttle him. "Pay what you owe me," he said. His fellow servant fell at his feet and implored him, saying, "Give me time and I will pay you." But the other would not agree; on the contrary, he had him thrown into prison till he should pay the debt. His fellow servants were deeply distressed when they saw what had happened, and they went to their master and reported the whole affair to him. Then the master sent for him. "You wicked servant," he said, "I cancelled all that debt of yours when you appealed to me. Were you not bound, then, to have pity on your fellow servant just as I had pity on you?"

—MATTHEW 18:21–33 (JB)

So then, if you are bringing your offering to the altar and there remember that your brother has something against you, leave your offering there before the altar, go and be reconciled with your brother first, and then come back and present your offering. —MATTHEW 5:23, 24 (JB)

forgive us our debts,
as we have forgiven those who are in debt to us.
—MATTHEW 6:12 (JB)

I'm sorry
  for offending people
  and then being hurt
  that they're offended
  and not caring
  or hoping
  quite enough
  to go and say
    I'm sorry"

I'm sorry
  for forgetting the kind things
  and remembering the cruel things
I'm sorry
  for being angry
  at the wrong time
  and not
  at the right time
I'm sorry
  for holding grudges
  and hugging bitterness

I'm sorry
  for neglecting my friend
  who needs affection
I'm sorry
  for not consulting my colleague
  who needs respect
I'm sorry
  for being sarcastic to my wife
  who needs understanding
I'm sorry
  for being critical of my daughter
  who needs appreciation
I'm sorry
  for being sorry for myself
  who needs love.

Touch And See

The people who walked in darkness
have seen a great light

Anna Filippi took a long stroll through a woods and a meadow today, and when it was over she said: "I liked it. It was a quiet place, and pretty well shaded. There were birds— it was peaceful. It was the type of walk you would take if you were not in a hurry. There were lots of things you could see."

Anna has been totally blind for all the sixteen years of her life. Her two walking companions today, Michael Turner, sixteen, and John Wilkinson, seventeen, have also been blind from birth. Because of this, they explored the new "touch and see" nature trail at the National Arboretum with a sensitivity and thoroughness that is rare for sighted people. The three of them spent an hour on the trail, almost alone. . . . They embraced the trunks of trees to feel their mightiness and their great age. They gathered in branches, sniffed bunches of leaves, listened to the crackle of twigs under their feet, and ran their fingers delicately over the bark of fallen logs. They perceived the density of the forest, and the openness of the meadow beyond. They were full of the wonder of their senses.

The three teen-agers followed the trail by sliding their hands along a continuous rope supported on posts. At intervals, they stopped at waist-high markers in Braille and print to read the inscriptions swiftly with their fingers. Then they would reach out for the nearby tree or shrub described on the marker to examine it with their hands and noses. The messages on the markers were not only botanical but also cautionary: "The trail now winds downhill. Hold firmly to guide rope"; aesthetic: "The leaves [of the white poplar] are fuzzy white underneath and dark shiny green above. They are fun to feel, and you can hear them flutter in the wind"; and philosophical: "Gradually decay organisms will begin to live and multiply in this log. After many years they will turn the wood into organic dust, and thus return this tree to the earth from which it grew. This cycle—life, growth, death and renewal—is the pattern of forest life, as of all life."

Michael fingered a willow down by the edge of the marsh and joked, "The marker says this thing is related to the weeping willow, but I don't hear anything—it must cry when it rains."

John wound his arms around the thick trunk of a white oak he had learned was eighty years old and exclaimed, "This is unbelievable!"

—NAN ROBERTSON

And there was a woman who had had a flow of blood for twelve years, and who had suffered much under many physicians and had spent all that she had, and was no better but rather grew worse.

She had heard the reports about Jesus, and came up behind him in the crowd and touched his garment.

For she said, "If I touch even his garments, I shall be made well."

And immediately the hemorrhage ceased; and she felt in her body that she was healed of her disease.

And Jesus said, "Who touched my garments?"

—MARK 5:25–34 (RSV)

Now Thomas, one of the twelve, called the Twin, was not with them when Jesus came.

So the other disciples told him, "We have seen the Lord." But he said to them, "Unless I see in his hands the print of the nails, and place my finger in the mark of the nails, and place my hand in his side, I will not believe."

Eight days later, his disciples were again in the house, and

Thomas was with them. The doors were shut, but Jesus came and stood among them, and said, "Peace be with you."

Then he said to Thomas, "Put your finger here, and see my hands; and put out your hand, and place it in my side; do not be faithless, but believing."

Thomas answered him, "My Lord and my God!"

Jesus said to him, "Have you believed because you have seen me? Blessed are those who have not seen and yet believe."

—JOHN 20:24–29 (RSV)

Seeing is believing. . . .
Believing is seeing. . . .

What's unbelievable:
that I could see and not believe, or
that I could not see and yet believe?

Is there a certain seeing
    which comes only by touching
        or being touched by
            trees and twigs?

Is there a certain seeing
    which comes only by touching
        or being touched by
            other people?

Can I touch You? Where, when?
Here, now?
That woman touched Jesus.
Thomas wanted to.
But did he?

Keep in touch with me.
Keep me in touch with my brothers.
Who's touching me?

Leaving Home

Open Letter

Sir:

Thank you for the excellent Essay "On Being An American Parent" (Dec. 15). Oh, how I wish every parent and future parent would read it and take it to heart! . . .

I love my parents and I know they love me, but they've ruined my life. . . . I could never tell my parents anything, it was always "I'm too busy . . . too tired . . . that's not important . . . that's stupid . . . can't you think of better things . . . oh, your friends are wrong . . . they're stupid." As a result, I stopped telling my parents anything. All communications ceased. We never had that very important thing—fun.

Oh, we had love. Prompted on my side by an ever-present fear of my mother and pity for my father, and prompted on their side by the thought that I was their responsibility and if I went wrong, they would be punished by God.

After four rotten years in a . . . girls' school (I did have two or three very wonderful teachers) I'm now stuck in an even worse . . . women's college. Only the best for me! They knew I didn't want to come but made me anyway. Their daughter wasn't going to be corrupted! I had already been saved from the evils of early dating and doing things that "everybody else" did. What is the result of this excellent upbringing? I'm 18 years old, drink whenever I get the chance, have smoked pot, and as of a very eventful Thanksgiving vacation, am no longer a virgin. Why? Was it my parents or just me? I'm so very confused—but who can I talk to? Not my parents. My parents could read this and never dream it was their daughter.

I have only one important plea to parents. . . . *Listen, listen, and listen again*. Please, I know the consequences and I'm in hell.

A COLLEGE STUDENT

—*Time*, December 22, 1967

Yahweh said to Abram, "Leave your country, your family, and your father's house, for the land I will show you. I will make you a great nation; I will bless you." . . . So Abram went. . . .   —GENESIS 12:1, 2, 4 (JB)

"Two men went up to the Temple to pray, one a Pharisee, the other a tax collector. The Pharisee stood there and said this prayer to himself, 'I thank you, God, that I am not grasping, unjust, adulterous like the rest of mankind, and particularly that I am not like this tax collector here. I fast twice a week; I pay tithes on all I get.' The tax collector stood some distance away, not daring even to raise his eyes to heaven; but he beat his breast and said, 'God, be merciful to me, a sinner.' "
                                              —LUKE 18:10–13 (JB)

In the course of their journey he came to a village, and a woman named Martha welcomed him into her house. She had a sister called Mary, who sat down at the Lord's feet and listened to him speaking. Now Martha who was distracted with all the serving said, "Lord, do you not care that my sister is leaving me to do the serving all by myself? Please tell her to help me." But the Lord answered, "Martha, Martha," he said, "you worry and fret about so many things, and yet few are needed, indeed only one. It is Mary who has chosen the better part; it is not to be taken from her."
                                              —LUKE 10:38–42 (JB)

> I feel for parents
>   who want to enjoy their children
>   but don't know how
>   who do their best
>   but fail
>   and don't know
>   why
>   it happened

I feel for kids
   who are no longer
   kids
   who want to enjoy their parents
   but can't
   who would rather stay home
   but have to leave
   or
   would rather leave home
   but have to stay
      in order to keep alive

Why is it so hard to listen?

Sometimes
when I try to listen
to my kids
I lose patience
   jump to conclusions
   criticize their friends
   don't understand
Sometimes
   I could cry
   we get so mad
            so quickly
   about so little

Maybe
   listening
   is the most important part of
   loving

Please!
   let me listen
   while there's still time
   before the kids start
                  leaving home

Intimations of Mortality

Please do not stand over me with promises of heaven when I lie dying. Although you would mean it well (and I thank you for that), my ears cannot receive it.

Your sight is no better than mine beyond the horizon of time and space. So I prefer my focus on this world in death as I have preferred it in life.

Remember with me near the end, if it is possible, that something of me will go on in humanity, that the good I have done does not have to be perfect to be effective, and that perhaps it will multiply in the lives of others, helping somehow in this amazing human endeavor.

And if I writhe knowing that the evil I have done will also live and possibly multiply, remind me that it is so with us all—not given in structure, but acquired unavoidably in patterns of life that conflict and hurt and destroy. . . .

Tell me, if you like, that I go into the arms of God, but you will add nothing to what I have been saying. You will be making poetry, as I have done in other words and ways.

Then let me go to nature as I came from nature, to the great cycles of creativity that I have dimly—so dimly—understood.

Do not, please, box me up in airtight compartments in a futile pretense against decay. Decay is a part of new life, the going as essential as the coming. Let me partake of it, my elements quickly and cooperatively entering into the grand chemical scheme of the universe that has sustained me from the moment of egg and sperm.

When you commit my ashes to the ground or to the stream, commit them! For then one cycle of individual life will be over and a unit of nature will be separated into its minute parts for participation in new ways, as atoms rearrange in the mysterious slow seething of the world. I have come from infinity and I go to infinity, between which events, for a little time, I came to celebrate that miracle which I could never fathom.

Therefore, when it is time (long, far from now, I hope) yield me dying, yield me dead in this tradition: earth to earth, ashes to ashes, dust to dust—in sure and certain hope that the dust which bloomed briefly in my loving will bloom again.

—MARY JEAN IRION

Indeed the fate of man and beast is identical; one dies, the other too, and both have the selfsame breath; man has no advantage over the beast, for all is vanity. Both go to the same place; both originate from the dust and to the dust both return. . . .

I see there is no happiness for man but to be happy in his work, for this is the lot assigned to him. Who then can bring him to see what is to happen after his time?

I come again to contemplate all the oppression that is committed under the sun. Take for instance the tears of the oppressed, with no one to protect them; the power their oppressors wield. No one to protect them! So, rather than the living who still have lives to live, I salute the dead who have already met death; happier than both of these is he who is yet unborn and has not seen the evil things that are done under the sun.

—ECCLESIASTES 3:19–4:3 (JB)

I think that what we suffer in this life can never be compared to the glory, as yet unrevealed, which is waiting for us. The whole creation is eagerly waiting for God to reveal his sons. . . . creation still retains the hope of being freed, like us, from its slavery to decadence, to enjoy the same freedom and glory as the children of God. From the beginning till now the entire creation, as we know, has been groaning in one great act of giving birth; and not only creation, but all of us who possess the first-fruits of the Spirit, we too groan inwardly as we wait for our bodies to be set free. . . .

With God on our side who can be against us? Since God did not spare his own Son, but gave him up to benefit us all we may be certain, after such a gift, that he will not refuse anything he can give. . . . Nothing therefore can come between us and the love of Christ, even if we are troubled or worried, or being persecuted, or lacking food or clothes, or being threatened or even attacked. . . . These are the trials through which we triumph, by the power of him who loved us. For I am certain of this: neither death nor life, no angel, no prince, nothing that exists, nothing still to come, not any power, or height or depth, nor any created thing, can ever come between us and the love of God made visible in Christ Jesus our Lord.

—ROMANS 8:18–19, 21–23, 31, 32, 35–39 (JB)

My dear people, we are already the children of God, but what we are to be in the future has not yet been revealed; all we know is, that when it is revealed, we shall be like him. . . .

—I JOHN 3:2 (JB)

From dust to dust—
    from infinity to infinity—are these
both ways of saying
    from nothing to nothing
    signifying nothing?

How can dust bloom again
except in poetry
unless there is something like
resurrection?

I think of the car-crushing machine
up whose inexorable ramp
old cars move

into whose mindless merciless maw
old cars go
to be mashed into metal
for the slag heap
      Is that the destiny
      of my beloved?
      If it is so
      I cannot pretend
      that I am content
      If it is so,
      I am sad and angry
      sad that Death destroys
        all truth, goodness, love, beauty, hope
        and people I love
      angry that there is no justice, ever,
        for the poor and the oppressed,
        and no mercy

          and no God

Is it naïve or
sentimental or
foolish to
hope that the arms of God
exist in reality deeper than
man's poetic imagination?
Then call me so
      For I refuse to believe that the
      grand chemical scheme of the universe
      is loveless and
        I will continue to
        hope
        that we shall be
        and
      that we shall be
      like him

On The Border of Two Worlds

This crow lives near my house, and though I have never injured him, he takes good care to stay up in the very highest trees and, in general, to avoid humanity. His world begins at about the limit of my eyesight.

On the particular morning when this episode occurred, the whole countryside was buried in one of the thickest fogs in years. The ceiling was absolutely zero. All planes were grounded, and even a pedestrian could hardly see his outstretched hand before him.

I was groping across a field in the general direction of the railroad station, following a dimly outlined path. Suddenly out of the fog, at about the level of my eyes, and so closely that I flinched, there flashed a pair of immense black wings and a huge beak. The whole bird rushed over my head with a frantic cawing outcry of such hideous terror as I have never heard in a crow's voice before, and never expect to hear again.

He was lost and startled, I thought, as I recovered my poise. He ought not to have flown out in this fog. He'd knock his silly brains out.

All afternoon that great awkward cry rang in my head. Merely being lost in a fog seemed scarcely to account for it—especially in a tough, intelligent old bandit such as I knew that particular crow to be. I even looked once in the mirror to see what it might be about me that had so revolted him that he had cried out in protest to the very stones.

Finally, as I worked my way homeward along the path, the solution came to me. It should have been clear before. The borders of our world had shifted. It was the fog that had done it. That crow, and I knew him well, never under normal circumstances flew low near men. He had been lost all right, but it was more than that. He had thought he was high up, and when he encountered me looming gigantically through the fog, he had perceived a ghastly and, to the crow mind, unnatural sight. He had seen a man walking on air, desecrating the very heart of the crow kingdom, a harbinger of the most profound evil a crow could conceive of—air-walking men. The encounter, he must have thought, had taken place a hundred feet over the roofs.

He caws now when he sees me leaving for the station in the morning, and I fancy that in that note I catch the uncertainty of a mind that has come to know things are not always what they seem. He has seen a marvel in his heights of air and is no longer as other crows. He has experienced the human world from an unlikely perspective. He and I share a viewpoint in common: our worlds have interpenetrated, and we both have faith in the miraculous.   —LOREN EISELEY

When evening came the boat was in the middle of the lake, while Jesus was alone on land. He saw that his disciples were having trouble rowing the boat, because the wind was blowing against them; so sometime between three and six o'clock in the morning he came to them, walking on the water. He was going to pass them by. But they saw him walking on the water. "It's a ghost!" they thought, and screamed. For when they all saw him they were afraid. Jesus spoke to them at once. "Take courage!" he said. "It is I. Don't be afraid!" Then he got into the boat with them, and the wind died down. The disciples were completely amazed and utterly confused.

—MARK 6:45–51 (TEV)

Moses was looking after the flock of Jethro, his father-in-law, priest of Midian. He led his flock to the far side of the wilderness and came to Horeb, the mountain of God. There the angel of Yahweh appeared to him in the shape of a flame of fire, coming from the middle of a bush. Moses looked; there was the bush blazing but it was not being burnt up. "I must go and look at this strange sight," Moses said, "and see why the bush is not burnt." Now Yahweh saw him go forward to look and God called to him from the middle of the bush. "Moses, Moses!" he said. "Here I am" he answered. "Come no nearer," he said. "Take off your shoes, for the place on which you stand is holy ground. I am the God of your father," he said, "the God of Abraham, the God of Isaac, and the God of Jacob." At this Moses covered his face, afraid to look at God. —EXODUS 3:1–6 (JB)

Saul kept up his violent threats of murder against the disciples of the Lord. He went to the High Priest and asked for letters of introduction to the Jewish meeting houses in Damascus, so that if he should find any followers of the Way of the Lord there, he would be able to arrest them, both men and women, and take them back to Jerusalem.

On his way to Damascus, as he came near the city, a light from the sky suddenly flashed all around him. He fell to the ground and heard a voice saying to him, "Saul, Saul! Why do you persecute me?" "Who are you, Lord?" he asked. "I am Jesus, whom you persecute," the voice said. "But get up and go into the city, where you will be told what you must do." Now the men who were traveling with Saul had stopped, not saying a word; they heard the voice but could not see anyone. Saul got up from the ground and opened his eyes, but could not see a thing. So they took him by the hand and led him into Damascus. For three days he was not able to see, and during that time he did not eat or drink anything.

—ACTS 9:1–9 (TEV)

I'm trying to figure out
what scares me

A friend wrote me
that he was angry
at something I did
and he is a peaceful man
and

I was shocked, then scared,
that I could get such a man
angry at me
Things were not
what they had seemed to be
I was not
what I had seemed to me
and to him
to be
My world was called
into question
I was called
into question

Do You meet me
in what scares me?

Is it You
who calls me
into question
and scares me
into the possibility
of becoming a blind man
who sees that he can't see

Fear of You
is the beginning
of wisdom, they say. . . .
Is it fear
of the unknown I'm in
or the unknown in me?

I'm Free to Be Who I Want

Two days before he refused to step forward in an Army induction center, an act that would have transformed him into Private Cassius Clay, Muhammad Ali sat in a Chicago motel coffee shop and moodily watched Lake Michigan roll beneath an April storm. . . .

Someone asked him why he didn't just play the game, go into the Army and give exhibitions and teach physical training like all the other major athletes? He leaned across the table, his eyes suddenly bright, and he spoke with great firmness: "What can you give me, America, for turning down my religion? How can I lose for standing up for Islam when presidents and princes invite me to their countries, when little people all over the East and Africa stop me in the street and say, 'Eat at my house, brother. Be an honor if you stay with us, brother'? You want me to give up all this love, America? You want me to do what the white man says and go fight a war against some people I don't know nothing about—get some freedom for some other people when my own people can't get theirs here? You want me to be so scared of the white man I'll go and get two arms shot off and 10 medals so you can give me a small salary and pat my head and say, 'Good boy, he fought for his country'?"

On April 28 in Houston, Muhammad stood his ground as he had promised. The reaction was unusually swift. Within hours, various boxing commissions summarily cashiered him as world heavyweight champion. Ten days later he was indicted by a Federal grand jury on a charge of refusing to submit to the draft, a felony punishable by 5 years in prison and a $10,000 fine. . . . He had become an official enemy of the people. The communications brokers who projected the ebullient Cassius Clay—and were thus trapped into maintaining the more serious Muhammad Ali—have always wondered why he didn't have the numb dignity of Joe Louis, the saccharine humility of Floyd Patterson or at least the darktown dash of Sugar Ray Robinson. They decided that Ali was just a misguided fool who had thrown away millions, a physical man enslaved by the dark powers of the Black Muslims. Perhaps it is hard to think of a barely literate, simple Negro athlete as a man of his times. . . .

. . . on February 26, 1964, the morning after he became champion, Clay confirmed the rumor of his Muslim membership . . . to a shocked and angry white press. Clay turned back their arguments with a soft and deadly, "I don't have to be what you want me to be. I'm free to be who I want."

As champion, he had a responsibility, he said, to provide a model for black youth. Unlike most athletic stars, he spent a great deal of time in the ghettos, walking the "little streets filled with little people." He shook hands with the wino, he said, because this would give the poor man a measure of self-respect. If he, the champ, shrank from the wino as did every one else, the man would just curl deeper into resentment and hopelessness.

In America, when facing hostility, he might be moved to snap back, in an extremely rare burst of mild profanity: "I get booed and this makes me strong. If everybody said, 'Oh, champ, you is wonderful,' I'd just lay back. But if a guy says, 'Son of a bitch, I hope you get your ass whipped,' I got to beat him and everybody else." But in London he could softly explain to African and Indian students that those who were against him "don't like me because I'm free. The Negro has always sold himself out for money or women, but I give up everything for what I believe. I'm a free man; I don't belong to nobody."

He spent 10 years of his life in sacrifice to a cause, the heavyweight championship, and his faith in himself was justified. No man could beat him, and when his title was taken away the New York Civil Liberties Union protested the action as arbitrary, capricious and unprincipled. Ali took another cause, that of a minority religion, and sacrificed again, giving up untold millions in revenue and divorcing a beautiful woman who would not abide by the sect's standards. Through it all, and under a constant pressure, he always did what he had to do, and never lost the almost magical purity that could believe, "ain't losing anything but gaining the world."

—ROBERT LIPSYTE

He called the people and his disciples to him, and said, "If anyone wants to be a follower of mine, let him renounce himself and take up his cross and follow me. For anyone who wants to save his life will lose it; but anyone who loses his life for my sake, and for the sake of the gospel, will save it. What gain, then, is it for a man to win the whole world and ruin his life?"

Great crowds accompanied him on his way and he turned and spoke to them, "If any man comes to me without hating his father, mother, wife, children, brothers, sisters, yes and his own life too, he cannot be my disciple."

—MARK 8:34–36; LUKE 14:25–26 (JB)

I swear by the living God who denies me justice,
    by Shaddai who has turned my life sour,
that as long as a shred of life is left in me,
    and the breath of God breathes in my nostrils,
my lips shall never speak untruth,
    nor any lie be found on my tongue.
Far from admitting you to be in the right:
    I will maintain my innocence to my dying day.
I take my stand on my integrity, I will not stir:
    my conscience gives me no cause to blush for my life.

—JOB 27:2–6 (JB)

How much longer will you forget me, Yahweh? For ever?
How much longer will you hide your face from me?
How much longer must I endure grief in my soul,
and sorrow in my heart by day and by night?
How much longer must my enemy have the upper hand of me?
Look and answer me, Yahweh my God!

Give my eyes light, or I shall sleep in death,
and my enemy will say, "I have beaten him,"
and my oppressors have the joy of seeing me stumble.
But I for my part rely on your love, Yahweh;
let my heart rejoice in your saving help.
Let me sing to Yahweh for the goodness he has shown to me.

—PSALM 113 (JB)

I'm free
to be
who
I want

integrity
    doing the truth
    conviction over convention
    faith against public opinion
    to my own self
    be true
    a minority of one
    may be
    right

sacrifice
    one can evade the draft by
    going to college or Canada
    one can resist by
    refusing induction

which means prison
there are more draft evaders than
draft resisters

freedom
   to be honest
   with myself
   and everybody else
freedom
   to be willing
   to lose everything but my
   soul
freedom
   to trust God
   with
   purity of heart

O God
free me
to be
who
I want

I Need Never Fear

I hear my father; I need never fear.

I hear my mother; I shall never be lonely, or want for love.

When I am hungry it is they who provide for me; when I am in dismay, it is they who fill me with comfort.

When I am astonished or bewildered, it is they who make the weak ground firm beneath my soul: it is in them that I put my trust.

When I am sick it is they who send for the doctor; when I am well and happy, it is in their eyes that I know best that I am loved; and it is towards the shining of their smiles that I lift up my heart and in their laughter that I know my best delight.

I hear my father and my mother and they are my giants, my king and my queen, beside whom there are no others so wise or worthy or honorable or brave or beautiful in this world.

I need never fear: nor ever shall I lack for lovingkindness.

—JAMES AGEE

The Lord is my shepherd, I shall not want;
   he makes me lie down in green pastures.
He leads me beside still waters;
   he restores my soul.
He leads me in the paths of righteousness
   for his name's sake.
Even though I walk through the valley of the shadow of death,
   I fear no evil;
for thou art with me;
   thy rod and thy staff,
   they comfort me.

—PSALM 23:1–4 (RSV)

At this time the disciples came to Jesus and said, "Who is the greatest in the kingdom of heaven?" So he called a little child to him and set the child in front of them. Then he said, "I tell you solemnly, unless you change and become like little children you will never enter the kingdom of heaven. And so, the one who makes himself as little as this little child is the greatest in the kingdom of heaven." —MATTHEW 18:1–4 (JB)

my three-year-old son
feels like that
about me
when I take him in my arms
he holds my face between his hands
and we look at each other
kisses are enough
to blow away
his tears

how amazing that he
trusts me
who am not
trustworthy

how awesome that
he thinks I am stronger than the
Monster
that mysterious power which would
hurt or
scare him
but even the Monster's power fades
when he is with me, for
I am his
father

Can I be like
my son
and
trust You
and not be
afraid

Interrogation

The road had widened into a little village and a crowd of soldiers had filled it. I walked forward into the group and pressed in among the figures and saw the black heap around which they circled. It fluttered! It was a man standing with two blankets hung over his head, one dragging crazily down his back into the snow. Then I saw the eyes, wild lights furtively flicking left and right, and the tongue moving over an indefinite mouth.

A Finnish officer came up to me and pointing with a helmet which he swished like a sickle, screamed, *"Ruske!"* I lost the rest in the unfamiliar language.

Two men with rifles were now prodding the prisoner forward. The little group waded over the snowbank and into a low-roofed wooden schoolhouse. For a moment after we brushed through the blackout blankets into the brightly lighted room we all stood like bats turning our heads toward sounds. Then we could see. School benches were piled one upon another in a heap on one side, blackboards with faint white images lined the other. A table with a bare electric bulb dangling above it stood in the center. Fifteen or eighteen officers and men, all heavily clothed, sat or stood about. On the table was a map, several automatic weapons, a nest of German grenades and a steaming teapot. Behind it sat a broad-shouldered Finnish major, his pale eyes impassive and his firm mouth controlled, neither stern nor smiling. Across the expressionless face a scar ran from ear to chin.

The Russian, still trailing his hood of blankets, was shoved before him and the major went into his interrogation without introduction. The replies came in dry whispers and the men in the room laughed loudly with every answer. He was forty-two, a dairy worker from Leningrad where he had a wife and three sons and a daughter. He thought—he struggled with himself to bring out the reply—he thought that his unit was on the Helsinki front. The room roared with laughter and the soldiers pounded their rifle butts on the floor. Kemi River was hundreds of miles north of where he thought he was.

The jeering audience was crowding forward and suddenly a soldier slipped up behind the prisoner and yanked the blankets from him. The Russian whirled with a tiny cry of fright. With a quick frown the major barked a command and his men moved back. Then, his face once more impassive, he paused before starting his questions again. When he did his voice was more gentle, almost soothing, and the interrogation was soon ended.

Reaching forward, he offered the prisoner a cigarette. The Russian stared at him and at the outstretched hand. His tongue, large and white, licked his cracked lips and he slowly raised two blackened and bloodstained hands toward the cigarette. He hesitated, then looked full into the eyes of the Finn. Suddenly tears welled down his dirt-cracked face and rolled off his encrusted, padded uniform. The room went silent. Gently the major placed the cigarette on the corner of the table and turned away as if to study the papers before him. For a long moment he sat withdrawn in silence while the Russian continued to tremble, his face now smeared where he had rubbed at the tears with the padded cuff.

I reached in my musette bag for my camera and flash gun. The major looked up. "You want to take his picture?" He beckoned to me. I stepped forward to move the Russian about facing the camera. He was rigid and shied from my touch like a mare. I turned him about and he moved slowly, reluctantly. I waved several soldiers out of the background and the prisoner watched me frantically. As he looked about and saw himself standing alone his knees sagged further and knocked audibly in the silent room.

"It's all right," I said assuringly. "I'm only taking your picture." But the major did not offer to translate. I held my camera aloft to show him but he only cringed away from me. Through the finder I saw his hands move up slightly in front of him and then drop. I flashed.

The Russian wheeled around, screaming. He sagged to his knees and grasped the table leg. There he remained, head pounding the table, weeping, stuttering Russian.

For a moment no one moved. Then, in shame, some of the officers and men slipped out of the room. The major jumped up and gently raised the sobbing prisoner. "You're not hurt," he repeated soothingly. "You're not hurt. We are not shooting you. We are taking your picture." He reached for my camera and held it to the Russian's wet face. "Look through the window." He spoke as one would speak to a child. "See through the window."

The furtive eyes flickered about the room. Then one eye caught the finder and two black hands reached up slowly and took hold of my camera. For a moment he peered through it at me and into the little group of Finns who waited quiet and embarrassed. Suddenly there was the flick of a smile, then a laugh. And then as the major held him he shook with screams of laughter.

Now the whole room was laughing and half a dozen hands were poking cigarettes at him. Someone put the blankets back over his head and we followed him out through the blackout curtains. Outside, the major turned him over to some guards and again he was surrounded by a gathering of soldiers in the moonlight.

—CARL MYDANS

. . . the men who guarded Jesus were mocking and beating him. They blindfolded him and questioned him. "Play the prophet," they said. "Who hit you then?" And they continued heaping insults on him. . . .

And they brought him before Pilate. They began their accusation by saying, "We found this man inciting our people to revolt, opposing payment of the tribute to Caesar, and claiming to be Christ, a king." Pilate put to him this question, "Are you the king of the Jews?" "It is you who say it," he replied. Pilate then said to the chief priests and the crowd, "I find no case against this man." But they persisted, "He is inflaming the people with his teaching all over Judea; it has come all the way from Galilee, where he started, down to here." . . .

Pilate then summoned the chief priests and the leading men and the people. "You brought this man before me," he said, "as a political agitator. Now I have gone into the matter myself in your presence and found no case against the man in respect of all the charges you bring against him. . . . As you can see, the man has done nothing that deserves death, so I shall have him flogged and then let go." But as one man they howled, "Away with him! Give us Barabbas!" (This man had been thrown into prison for causing a riot in the city and for murder.)

Pilate was anxious to set Jesus free and addressed them again, but they shouted back, "Crucify him! Crucify him!" And for the third time he spoke to them, "Why? What harm has this man done? I have found no cause against him that deserves death, so I shall have him punished and then let him go." But they kept on shouting at the top of their voices, demanding that he should be crucified. And their shouts were growing louder.

Pilate then gave his verdict: their demand was to be granted. He released the man they asked for, who had been imprisoned for rioting and murder, and handed Jesus over to them to deal with as they pleased.

—LUKE 22:63–65; 23:2–5, 13–25 (JB)

Something there is in me
       that makes for a mob
something cowardly
       that gangs up on a man
       when he's down
       especially an enemy,
                   or competitor
                   or outsider

Something there is in me
       that puts a finger to the wind
something cold
       that washes my hands of a loser
       and gives the people
       what they want

Something there is in me
       that defends
       the defenseless
something tough
       that comes out tender
       to comfort the casualty
       or protect the protester

it's cruel
but common
       to play cat and mouse
       with people
it's cruel
but common
       to be on the carpet
       and have the rug pulled out
       to be at bay
           before a boss
               or a board

a prisoner
discovers his own mettle
in the moment of
interrogation
       when truth
       is sought
       or bought
          by terror

Am I a prisoner?
Who interrogates me?
Whom do I interrogate?

The truth
that a man is
becomes visible
when Power
has him by the
throat

We're All with You, David

Thirty-six business executives are gathered together in a resort hotel for three days. They are there to learn to "level" with one another in ways previously unknown to them in the office environment of the aerospace company for which they work. Divided into three groups, the men spent several hours together the first day, in informal attire with no indication of rank. The men in Group One began to open up and express their feelings, needling, sparring, joking. The group began to find the strength of a new intimacy, pressuring first one member, then another, into the center of the ring.

The next morning, without warning, it broke. Full of breakfast, bored by a dull general session, Group One was still settling into its room when Paul, a Texas salesman, started trading conversation with David. "You know some writers," Paul said. "What's your idea of a good communicator?"

"Oh, I don't know," David mused. "Underneath everything like technique, I guess if you're going to make a difference—a positive one—in the world, you have to be a good person. . . ."

"So how would you define that?"

"It's more than just a nice guy. I mean a *good* man, someone who cares. . . ." Startled by the intensity he felt, David caught a winging panicky question in the corner of his mind's eye: "Is this my time? . . . The group instinct picked up a signal from somewhere inside him. Chatter stopped. They waited.

"I want to be a good man," he said, choosing words slowly. "That means changing the world, making it a less wasteful place. I can't just rattle through my job, take the money, go home and tune out. . . .

"Sometimes you'd think everybody is crazy. . . ." He stared at the light of the window: ". . . flinging incredible amounts of energy around, everywhere you look . . . wasted. We do such violence to each other. We're fighting wars . . . race, we're fighting each other, scaring children at school, scaring them at home. . . . Nobody could do any of it if they weren't so locked up inside of themselves, out of touch with the people they hurt. God, I hate all that violence . . ." He almost stopped, but the pressure to make the group understand was too great.

"I almost killed the person I love the most, last year, because I got sealed up inside. My wife and I are one person, closer than I know how to tell you. But it still happened. . . . We were at a music festival up the coast. We'd taken our seven-year-old son along, and . . . I don't know, various little things happened that bothered me, and I built up a bad mood. . . . Sunday afternoon, I wanted more than anything for us to hear Ali Akbar Khan play the sarod. Well, we had to give up our seat in front and sit outside the door, listening to a loudspeaker. . . . My wife went off several times during the music to look for our boy . . . I just got madder and madder until I said something bitter to her. I don't even remember what it was, but she told me I was a genius at causing pain. We walked out on the grass. I said she was stupid to get mad at *me*. . . . She told me to leave her alone, and . . . and . . . she said it in a way that froze me, as if she meant to cut me off from her. That had never happened before. I was terrified. I didn't know what to do. . . . So I guess I started trying to hurt her."

David tried to dry his eyes with a handkerchief.

"I grabbed her arm as hard as I could, dug in my fingers so they would bruise her through her parka . . . pushed her down a dirt path away from the music. She was crying. Everything in me was focused on my fingers crushing her arm. We got to the end of the path, and she kept saying, 'Let me go, let me go' . . ."

Swimming in the memory, he bowed his head and let the tears fall on his knees as he spoke to his unseen group.

"I started saying, 'Listen, damn it, listen, don't try to run away,' and I grabbed her by the shoulders. I can remember her eyes, so wide, staring . . . I started shaking her, but my right hand slipped as I pushed her back and forth, and smashed her in the throat."

He smacked his Adam's apple hard.

"She said the strangest thing. 'Wait a minute,' she said. . . . 'Wait a minute,' like in a theater when you want to go back over a line. Then she couldn't breathe, couldn't talk, and I thought I had broken her windpipe. I thought she was going to die. . . . Everything inside me broke. I held her in my arms and cried and said, 'I'm sorry, I'm sorry, I love you . . .' How could I kill her? What happened to me? . . .

"She got back a little breath after a few minutes. I was so thankful she was all right. But you see what I mean about waste? Hurting? . . ."

Chris had been staring at the rug. He looked up, showing tears of his own, and reached out a hand. "David . . . David," he said, "I want you to know I really feel for you. I'm with you . . ." David nodded, unable to speak.

Matt said softly, "We're all with you, David." Lehner, Paul, Bruce, others murmured assent. Some stared out the window. Others studied their hands.

Silence. David sat passive, clean and open, unarmored, feeling closer to the group than he had before, not because he knew them but because they knew him. He floated free, ready to respond to the lightest touch. They would not hurt him.

—JOHN POPPY

Then Joseph could not control himself before all those who stood by him; and he cried, "Make every one go out from me." So no one stayed with him when Joseph made himself known to his brothers. And he wept aloud, so that the Egyptians heard it, and the household of Pharaoh heard it. And Joseph said to his brothers, "I am Joseph; is my father still alive?" But his brothers could not answer him, for they were dismayed at his presence.

So Joseph said to his brothers, "Come near to me, I pray you." And they came near. And he said, "I am your brother, Joseph, whom you sold into Egypt. . . ."

Then he fell upon his brother Benjamin's neck and wept; and Benjamin wept upon his neck. And he kissed all his brothers and wept upon them; and after that his brothers talked with him.   —GENESIS 45:1–4, 14–15 (RSV)

But the harvest of the Spirit is love, joy, peace, patience, kindness, goodness, fidelity, gentleness, and self-control. There is no law dealing with such things as these. . . .

We must not be conceited, challenging one another to rivalry, jealous of one another. If a man should do something wrong, my brothers, on a sudden impulse, you who are endowed with the Spirit just set him right again very gently. Look to yourself, each one of you: you may be tempted too. Help one another to carry these heavy loads, and in this way you will fulfill the law of Christ.   —GALATIANS 5:22–23, 26; 6:2 (NEB)

How good, how delightful it is
    for all to live together like brothers:

fine as oil on the head,
    running down the beard,
running down Aaron's beard
    to the collar of his robes;

copious as a Hermon dew
    falling on the heights of Zion,
where Yahweh confers his blessing,
    everlasting life.
                    —PSALM 133 (JB)

I want to be a good man
someone who cares
Why do I hurt the people I love?
I haven't cried for a long time
except a few tears
in a movie,
not really cried
out of my guts
I wish I could reveal
myself
to others
But I'm afraid
to be known—why?
I give time and energy and money
but
withhold myself
There never seems to be
time
or place,
or people
when I can share
what I fear . . . about myself. . . .
I wish there were

Everyman Wants to Hit Hard

He wasn't leading. He wasn't even close to leading. He had won only one tournament this year and he stood only 22d on the official money-winning list.

But the largest gallery at the Westchester Country Club today belonged to Arnold Palmer. The largest galleries at golf tournaments everywhere belong to Arnold Palmer. And in this case, belong is almost the precise word because the fierce loyalty of Palmer's supporters, aptly named Arnie's Army, is a phenomenon of modern sports.

Why Palmer's? The reasons are many and complex and maybe only a psychiatrist could find them all.

Basically, Palmer is a fine golfer. He plays the type of game every hacker wishes he could play. And perhaps most important, Palmer has the quality that might best be described as animal magnetism.

- Willie Mays has it, but not Mickey Mantle.
- Bill Russell has it, but not Wilt Chamberlain.
- Pancho Gonzales has it, but not Ken Rosewall.
- Valery Brumel has it, but not Randy Matson.
- Sugar Ray Robinson has it, but not Floyd Patterson.

In golf, despite dozens of heroes created on the tour and nurtured by television, only Palmer has it.

Jack Nicklaus has a cherubic smile and awe-inspiring strength, but he is liked rather than revered. Gary Player is too small to be Everyman's hero. Ben Hogan, in his heydey, was respected but impersonal.

There is nothing impersonal about Palmer.

When Palmer is happy, his face lights up. When Palmer is thinking, he frowns. When he plays a bad shot, he scowls, and the world hates the ball that betrayed him. His emotions are never in doubt.

People who see Palmer for the first time are often surprised. At 5 feet 10½ inches, he is shorter than many expect. At 185 pounds, he is heavier than many expect. He has the shoulders and biceps of a blacksmith.

He moves around a golf course like a caged tiger. He doesn't walk, he attacks. When he addresses the ball, his muscles tighten and his face reddens. And then he does what Everyman wants to do on every shot—he murders the ball.

This, perhaps, is the closest bond of all. Everyman wants to hit hard, as if this alone is the secret of successful golf. Sam Snead may have a picture swing, but Arnold Palmer just murders the ball.

Everyman simply cannot hit a golf ball so far and so well as does Palmer. Everyman also cannot be so physically uninhibited and yet emotionally honest.

When Palmer makes a bad shot, he is the first to announce it. He makes no excuses. At the same time, he asks no one to suffer his pains. It is a manly combination of qualities, and his devotees love him all the more for it.

In short, only a baseball player can be Willie Mays, only a fighter can be Sugar Ray Robinson. But every golfer can be Arnold Palmer because Arnold Palmer is every golfer.

—FRANK LITSKY

Whenever David went out, on whatever mission Saul sent him, he was successful, and Saul put him in command of the fighting men; he stood well in the people's eyes and in the eyes of Saul's officers too.

On their way back, as David was returning from killing the Philistine, the women came out to meet King Saul from all the towns of Israel, singing and dancing to the sound of tambourine and lyre and cries of joy; and as they danced the women sang:

"Saul has killed his thousands,
and David his tens of thousands."

Saul was very angry; the incident was not to his liking. "They have given David the tens of thousands," he said, "but me only the thousands; he has all but the kingship now." And Saul turned a jealous eye on David from that day forward. . . .

—I SAMUEL 18:5–9, 15, 16 (JB)

65

. . . he saw James Son of Zebedee and his brother John; they too were in their boat, mending their nets. He called them at once and, leaving their father Zebedee in the boat with the men he employed, they went after him.

They went as far as Capernaum, and as soon as the sabbath came he went to the synagogue and began to teach. And his teaching made a deep impression on them because, unlike the scribes, he taught them with authority. . . .

Jesus withdrew with his disciples to the lakeside, and great crowds from Galilee followed him. From Judea, Jerusalem, Idumaea, Transjordania and the region of Tyre and Sidon, great numbers who had heard of all he was doing came to him. And he asked his disciples to have a boat ready for him because of the crowd, to keep him from being crushed. For he had cured so many that all who were afflicted in any way were crowding forward to touch him. . . .

. . . they took the colt to Jesus and threw their cloaks on its back and he sat on it. Many people spread their cloaks on the road, others greenery which they had cut in the fields. And those who went in front and those who followed were all shouting, "Hosanna! Blessings on him who comes in the name of the Lord! Blessings on the coming kingdom of our father David!"
—MARK 1:19–22; 3:7–9; 11:7–10 (JB)

Palmer murders the ball
David kills his tens of thousands
Jesus teaches with authority
   and the people love them for it

And what of me?
Am I like Saul:
   jealous, angry, frightened
   at another man's
   success

unwilling to share
the people's affection
with another

No man wants to be
second best
Everyman wants to be first
or at least
first among equals

Everyman wants to hit hard
I do
Everyman wants to defeat his enemies
I do
Everyman wants to be loved by the people
I do

And yet
no man can be everything
he wants to be
at least
not all the time
I can't

Help me
    to admire the success of other men
    without resentment
    or envy
Help me
    to hit as hard as I can
    with exultation
    and joy
Help me
    to be the man
    I have it in me to be

Songs in the Night

Let the children come to me . . .
for to such belong the kingdom of God.

October

Dear Friends,

Our Stevie was a special gift from God to us. He was given a good, strong body, a fine and inquisitive mind, and a warm and sensitive heart for people and for animals. His last task from his hospital bed was finding a good family for each one of his six curly black-haired puppies.

We were so proud of our gallant little fellow who fought so bravely. "Please read to me, Mommie, from my Bible of the miracles which Jesus did," he used to say, "You know, Daddy, when it hurts so much and I become afraid, I pray and ask God for courage and he always helps me to get through."

The time was short. His Daddy took him on Thursday, September 12, to the hospital. He had one completely collapsed lung. For ten days, the lung specialist tried to restore the lung to activity, but was hindered by a tumor which gave reason for suspicion. An exploratory operation of the abdomen confirmed that our Stevie suffered from a very malignant, fast-growing cancer which had invaded his whole system. On Saturday morning, September 28, both of us, in a circle of love and prayers, accompanied our son to the entrance of this other existence, where pain and sadness have lost their power.

On Sunday morning early, Richard discovered in our yard a beautiful orchid blossom. We had brought those plants from Hawaii, but the California climate was not suitable for them. So many times Richard had admonished Stevie to water them more often, but they seemed so sad and dry to us that we had given up hope on them—and then appeared this beautiful blossom on the day of Stevie's departure and a second one on the day of his burial. It was to us like Stevie's laughter, saying to us in his witty way, "Dad, the joke is on you. Life has more power than death."

The Memorial Service was held in the Chapel of Friendship at the Spanish American Institute. Rev. Melvin Talbert, our Superintendent, directed our eyes to the life everlasting and when he asked, "Will we see our loved one again?", Markus, who is very lonely for Stevie, nodded his head vigorously in affirmation. A friend sang a part from "Amahl and the Night Visitors" which Stevie loved to sing with his good, clear voice. Hymns of faith resounded in the Chapel and something wonderful, like the joy and victory of Easter morning, entered our hearts. Yes, our God can give songs in the night.

We buried our son on a lovely hillside at the Green Hills Memorial Park in San Pedro. His Dad, who had consecrated him at the altar as a baby and baptized him when he asked for it as a six-year-old, committed his body to the earth. There, on the lofty hillside, Heidi and Markie and we, his parents, sang him his beloved round, "The Lord's my Shepherd, I walk with him always."

—RICHARD and LEAN ACOSTA
with HEIDI and MARKIE

When my soul is downcast within me,
    I think of you;
from the land of Jordan and of Hermon,
    of you, humble mountain!

Deep is calling to deep
    as your cataracts roar;
all your waves, your breakers,
    have rolled over me.

In the daytime may Yahweh

command his love to come,
and by night may his song be on my lips,
    a prayer to the God of my life!
                    —PSALM 42:6–8 (JB)

How I love your palace,
    Yahweh Sabaoth!
How my soul yearns and pines
    for Yahweh's courts!
My heart and my flesh sing for joy
    to the living God.

The sparrow has found its home at last,
the swallow a nest for its young,
your altars, Yahweh Sabaoth,
    my king and my God.

Happy those who live in your house
    and can praise you all day long;
and happy the pilgrims inspired by you
    with courage to make the Ascents!

As they go through the Valley of the Weeper
    they make it a place of springs,
clothed in blessings by early rains.
Thence they make their way from height to height,
soon to be seen before God on Zion.

Yahweh Sabaoth, hear my prayer,
listen, God of Jacob;
God, our shield, now look on us
and be kind to your anointed.

A single day in your courts
    is worth more than a thousand elsewhere. . . .
                    —PSALM 84:1–10 (JB)

You shall have a song as in the night when a holy feast is kept; and gladness of heart, as when one sets out to the sound of the flute to go to the mountain of the Lord. . . .

—ISAIAH 30:29 (RSV)

How can they make it
from the valley of weeping
to the mountain of the Lord?
How can they sing songs
in the night
the terrible night?
I couldn't do it
I can't do it

Cancer in a little boy:
my boy?

Life has more power than death:
does it?
We will see our loved ones again:
will we?

a little child shall lead them

be with me
in my valley
and lead me
to Your mountain

Something Went "Click"

Not long ago Dr. Gattegno taught a demonstration class at Lesley-Ellis School. I don't believe I will ever forget it. It was one of the most extraordinary and moving spectacles I have seen in all my life.

The subjects chosen for this particular demonstration were a group of severely retarded children. There were about five or six 14- or 15-year olds. Some of them, except for unusually expressionless faces, looked quite normal; the one who caught my eye was a boy at the end of the table. He was tall, pale, with black hair. I have rarely seen on a human face such anxiety and tension as showed on his. He kept darting looks around the room like a bird, as if enemies might come from any quarter left unguarded for more than a second. His tongue worked continuously in his mouth, bulging out first one cheek and then the other. Under the table, he scratched—or rather clawed—at his leg with one hand. He was a terrifying and pitiful sight to see.

With no formalities or preliminaries, no ice-breaking or jollying up, Gattegno went to work. First he took two blue rods, and between them put a dark green, so that between the two blue and above the dark green there was an empty space 3 cm long. He said to the group, "Make one like this." They did. Then he said, "Now find the rod that will just fill up that space." I don't know how the other children worked on the problem; I was watching the dark-haired boy. His movements were spasmodic, feverish. When he had picked a rod out of the pile in the center of the table, he could hardly stuff it in between his blue rods. After several trials, he and the others found that a light green rod would fill the space.

Then Gatterno, holding his blue rods at the upper end, shook them, so that after a bit the dark green rod fell out. Then he turned the rods over, so that now there was a 6 cm. space where the dark green rod had formerly been. He asked the class to do the same. They did. Then he asked them to find the rod that would fill that space. Did they pick out of the pile the dark green rod that had just come out of that space? Not one did. Instead, more trial and error. Eventually, they all found that the dark green rod was needed.

Hard as it may be to believe, Gattefino went through this at least four or five times before anyone was able to pick the needed rod without hesitation and without trial and error. As I watched, I thought, "What must it be like to have so little idea of the way the world works, so little feeling for the regularity, the orderliness, the sensibleness of things?" It takes a great effort of the imagination to put oneself back, back to the place where we knew as little as these children. It is not just a matter of not knowing this fact or that fact; it is a matter of living in a universe like the one lived in by very young children, a universe which is utterly whimsical and unpredictable, where nothing has anything to do with anything else—with this difference, that these children had come to feel, as most very young children do not, that this universe is an enemy.

Then, as I watched, the dark-haired boy *saw!* Something went "click" inside his head, and for the first time, his hand visibly shaking with excitement, he reached without trial and error for the right rod. He could hardly stuff it into the empty space. It worked! The tongue going round in the mouth, and the hand clawing away at the leg under the table doubled their pace. When the time came to turn the rods over and fill the other empty space, he was almost too excited to pick up the rod he wanted; but he got it in. "It fits, it fits!" he said, and held up the rods for all of us to see. Many of us were moved to tears, by his excitement and joy, and by our realization of the great leap of the mind he had just taken.

—JOHN HOLT

Now Peter and John were going up to the temple at the hour of prayer, the ninth hour. And a man lame from birth was being carried, whom they laid daily at that gate of the temple which is called Beautiful to ask alms of those who entered the temple. Seeing Peter and John about to go into the temple, he asked for alms. And Peter directed his gaze at him, with John, and said, "Look at us." And he fixed his attention upon them, expecting to receive something from them. But Peter said, "I have no silver and gold, but I give you what I have; in the name of Jesus Christ of Nazareth, walk." And he took him by the right hand and raised him up; and immediately his feet and ankles were made strong. And leaping up he stood and walked and entered the temple with them, walking and leaping and praising God. And all the people saw him walking and praising God, and recognized him as the one who sat for alms at the Beautiful Gate of the temple; and they were filled with wonder and amazement at what had happened to him.

—ACTS 3:1–10 (RSV)

I remember you in my prayers, and ask the God of our Lord Jesus Christ, the glorious father, to give you the Spirit, who will make you wise and reveal God to you, so that you will know him. I ask that your minds may be opened to see his light, so that you will know what is the hope to which he has called you, how rich are the wonderful blessings he promises to his people, and how very great is his power at work in us who believe. This power in us is the same as the mighty strength which he used when he raised Christ from death. . . .   —EPHESIANS 1:16–20 (TEV)

Sometimes
I feel
like a
retarded child
nothing fits
I'm a misfit
there's so much
I don't understand
the universe seems
hostile to me
You are my
enemy

Sometimes
in my mind
something goes "click"
and I see!
for a beautiful moment
I see
things fit
I fit in
I understand
the universe seems
kind to me
You are my
friend

Please
give me more of those
beautiful moments
don't give up on me
be patient
keep teaching me until I
        touch truth
        handle hope
let me learn
from my own failures
if necessary, but
let me learn
and grow

awaken my hope
tap my creativity
open up new worlds
        of meaning
        for me
that I may
know the hope
to which You are calling
me
then I will leap for joy!

Happiness Is

The Gorths have found happiness through faith in television. "Absolute faith in the doctrine of materialism as revealed on Channels 2, 4, 5, 7, 9, and 20," says Bill, "has made a new person of me."

"Fabulous," says Cora Sue. "Twice as much happiness power as my old faith product."

Bill's conversion began one day when, listless, Vietnam-weary and tired of his marriage, he sat in the evening traffic jam slouched at the wheel of his Hupmobile. "Suddenly," he says, "I realized that it wasn't happening. When I got home that night I told Cora Sue, 'We've got to find something that will make it happen.' That night Channel 4 spoke to me for the first time. 'Rhinoceros makes it happen,' Channel 4 said." . . .

Seeing Bill's new happiness, Cora Sue began taking instruction from Channel 9. One night after Bill had hitched his Rhinoceros at the curb and fought off the beauties swarming to kiss him, he entered the kitchen to find Cora Sue wearing a Queen's crown. That afternoon, on instruction from Channel 9, she had quit greasing the bread with the high-priced spread and had switched to new improved gummoid margarine.

Since that day both Gorths have become contented, if somewhat hysterical, people. This gives an odd quality to attempts to make conversation with them. Commonplace conversational gambits such as, "Why am I so miserable all the time?" bring answers such as, "It's that old product you're using on your hair, friend."

"Fabulous," says Cora Sue. "Twice as much anti-misery power, too."

Like so many converts, the Gorths have no patience with skeptics. "What! Not believe in the new washday miracle?" Bill will ask. "Why, man, you might as well deny the existence of twice as much anti-perspirant power. You might as well say there is no crunchy goodness flavor-packed into every wholesome kernel of springtime freshness."

Nothing irritates Bill Gorth more than someone's pointing out that he talks like a fool. "Of course I talk like a fool," he says. "Cora Sue and I both talk like fools. It is our way of being absolutely loyal to our beliefs. Look, this whole neighborhood, this whole city, this whole country is swarming with people who practice the same faith we do. The only difference is that they're ashamed of it. It conceals their shame if they can laugh at the language of the channels, but it doesn't stop them from living by the message. Cora Sue and I believe in being perfectly honest about our faith."

"Fabulous," says Cora Sue. "Twice as much fool-exposure power, too."

Happiness to Bill and Cora Sue is belief in faster starting, brighter laundry, quicker relief, fresher smoke, longer protection, shinier floors, crunchier goodness, crispier chips, sexier lips, slimmer hips and happier trips.

"As a religion," says Bill, "I'll admit it's not much, but at least it is suited to today's world."

"Fabulous," says Cora Sue. "Twice as much fun as that old moralizing, too."　　　　　　　　　　　　　—RUSSELL BAKER

In that day the Lord will take away the finery of the anklets, the headbands, and the crescents; the pendants, the bracelets, and the scarfs; the headdresses, the armlets, the sashes, the perfume boxes, and the amulets; the signet rings and nose rings; the festal robes, the mantles, the cloaks, and the handbags; the garments, the turbans, and the veils.

Instead of perfume there will be rottenness;
　　and instead of a girdle, a rope;
and instead of well-set hair, baldness;
　　and instead of a rich robe, a girding of sackcloth;
　　instead of beauty, shame.　　　　—ISAIAH 3:16–24 (RSV)

How happy are the poor in spirit:
theirs is the kingdom of heaven.
Happy the gentle:
they shall have the earth for their heritage.
Happy those who mourn:
they shall be comforted.
Happy those who hunger and thirst for what is right:
they shall be satisfied.
Happy the merciful:
they shall have mercy shown them.
Happy the pure in heart:
they shall see God.
Happy the peacemakers:
they shall be called sons of God.
Happy those who are persecuted in the cause of right:
theirs is the kingdom of heaven.

—MATTHEW 5:3–10 (JB)

Happiness is
 the family in the car singing
 listening to my daughter tell
  what happened at school
  and looking at her.
 the sound of music anytime
  and of birdsong in the morning
 after work
  before dinner
   a drink
 reading to my son
  and watching him play trucks
 talking things over with my wife
 making love
 having even a small part in
  aiding the revolution of the
  young, black, and poor
 money in the bank

a fresh idea
when my work is productive
sharing someone's joy or trouble
When I am glad to be me
    without apology or envy
when I believe in
    You
when I let others be who they are
    without coercion or condemnation
making plans
being at peace with my colleagues
discovering a beautiful view
    and feasting my eyes on it
getting through a tough time
blasting the establishment!
thick sideburns, full beards, and miniskirts
the congregation
    really belting out a great hymn
a long walk at night
being willing
    to let life shape me
    as well as
    trying to shape life
invitations
making my parents happy
winning
a letter from a friend
water-skiing on one ski
people who are not defensive
me when I'm not defensive

and lots more. . . .
    thanks, Lord!

    happiness does not yield her charms to
        pur-suiters
    the declaration notwithstanding

The Silent Father

"When I was very young, my father, may he rest in peace, began to wake me in the middle of the night, just so I would cry. I was a child, but he would wake me and tell me stories about the destruction of Jerusalem and the sufferings of the people of Israel, and I would cry. For years he did this. Once he took me to visit a hospital—ah, what an experience that was!—and often he took me to visit the poor, the beggars, to listen to them talk. My father himself never talked to me, except when we studied together. He taught me with silence. He taught me to look into myself, to find my own strength, to walk around inside myself in company with my soul. When his people would ask him why he was so silent with his son, he would say to them that he did not like to talk, words are cruel, words play tricks, they distort what is in the heart, they conceal the heart, the heart speaks through silence. One learns of the pain of others by suffering one's own pain, he would say, by turning inside oneself, by finding one's own soul. And it is important to know of pain, he said. It destroys our self-pride, our arrogance, our indifference toward others. It makes us aware of how frail and tiny we are and of how much we must depend upon the Master of the Universe. Only slowly, very slowly, did I begin to understand what he was saying. For years his silence bewildered and frightened me, though I always trusted him, I never hated him. And when I was old enough to understand, he told me that of all people a tzaddik* especially must know of pain. A tzaddik must know how to suffer for his people, he said. He must take their pain from them and carry it on his own shoulder. He must cry, in his heart he must always cry. Even when he dances and sings, he must cry for the sufferings of his people."

—CHAIM POTOK

*A righteous, wiseman.

And Abraham took the wood of the burnt offering, and laid it on Isaac his son; and he took in his hand the fire and the knife. So they went both of them together. And Isaac said to his father Abraham, "My father!" And he said, "Here am I, my son." He said, "Behold, the fire and the wood; but where is the lamb for a burnt offering?" Abraham said, "God will provide himself the lamb for a burnt offering, my son." So they went both of them together.

When they came to the place of which God had told him, Abraham built an altar there, and laid the wood in order, and bound Isaac his son, and laid him on the altar, upon the wood. Then Abraham put forth his hand, and took the knife to slay his son. But the angel of the Lord called to him from heaven, and said, "Abraham, Abraham!" And he said, "Here am I." He said, "Do not lay your hand on the lad or do anything to him; for now I know that you fear God, seeing you have not withheld your son, your only son, from me." And Abraham lifted up his eyes and looked, and behold, behind him was a ram, caught in a thicket by his horns; and Abraham went and took the ram, and offered it up as a burnt offering instead of his son. So Abraham called the name of that place The Lord will provide. . . .   —GENESIS 22:6–14 (RSV)

He then left to make his way as usual to the Mount of Olives, with the disciples following. When they reached the place he said to them, "Pray not to be put to the test." Then he withdrew from them, about a stone's throw, and knelt down and prayed. "Father," he said, "if you are willing, take this cup away from me. Nevertheless, let your will be done, not mine." Then an angel appeared to him, coming from heaven to give him strength. In his anglish he prayed even more earnestly, and his sweat fell to the ground like great drops of blood. When he rose from prayer he went to the disciples and found them sleeping from sheer grief.

—LUKE 22:39–45 (JB)

Is it You
who wakes me
in the darkness
to cry
without tears

Is it You
who forces me
to learn
through my own pain
of the pain
of others

You are cruel
to teach me
with silence
I am afraid
of silence
I want
answers, reasons
But You are silent
not absent
but silent
Why?
Will you kill me
with silence
my father?

Yet
You do not leave me
     alone
You come to me
You strengthen me
You provide for me
You do not remove
     my pain or fear
     but
You help me bear it
     and grow tender
You are teaching me
to trust You
     in the silence
and I am learning

                              so slowly

there is kindness
in your cruelty

I hear You
in the sounds of
silence

Kishan Babu

Mr. and Mrs. Kishan Babu and their two children live at a respectable address on Central Avenue in Calcutta, the site of a middle-class apartment house. But they would not normally be considered either respectable or middle-class, for they live outside, on the sidewalk.

Every night at about 10 o'clock Kishan and his family spread some matting on the same patch of sidewalk under the same portico. About 40 persons are there—the same 40 every night. Most of them, like Kishan Babu and his young wife, Lila, were born in Calcutta and grew up in its streets. They have never lived indoors.

Everyone in Kishan Babu's cluster pursues the same trade—one of the oddest, more marginal occupations known to this city in which productive work is even harder to find than a home.

It is a three-stage operation, requiring plenty of enterprise. First they buy stainless steel pots from a wholesaler on credit. Then they go from door to door in middle class neighborhoods and exchange the pots for old clothes. Finally, they sell the old clothes, and pay the wholesaler.

In this way, Kishan Babu and his wife clear 4 or 5 rupees a day (about 60 cents). They are always able to select their clothes from what they collect along the way and their earnings are enough, barely, for their food.

Their only other major expense is the rent they pay for a locker, or stall, in a shanty on the other side of the avenue. It is five feet square, with a low metal roof that leaks and a damp dirt floor. It is here that they cook their evening meal over a wood fire. It was also here that Lila gave birth to her two children, Dillip and Maya.

To understand why the Babus choose to sleep on the sidewalk instead of indoors, it is only necessary to visit the stall. The visitor regains the street with a deep sense of relief.

Most sidewalk dwellers, all but those who are completely down and out, have some tiny roofed space they can call their own, even if it is not inhabitable. It is this that gives them their legal existence; the address they need to qualify for a ration card, a vote or a place in school for their children. Kishan Babu is determined his children go to school, as he himself did for a year.

But he has little hope that he will be able to rescue his family from the sidewalk, something his own father never managed. "How can I?" he asks. "What is left after I pay the rent on that room you saw and buy the food for my family?"

This year the answer has been less than nothing. Food prices are higher in Calcutta now than ever before and Lila Babu's one gold earring—the family's most valued possession —is held by the pot wholesaler, to whom they owe 80 rupees, nearly $11.

All India is prayerfully waiting now for a good harvest, which would reduce food prices. For Kishan Babu that would mean an opportunity to recover his wife's earring. Otherwise his life will go on as before.

—JOSEPH LELYVELD

Do not be worried about the food and drink you need to stay alive, or about clothes for your body. After all, isn't life worth more than food? and isn't the body worth more than clothes? Look at the birds flying around: they do not plant seeds, gather a harvest, and put it into barns; your Father in heaven takes care of them! Aren't you worth much more than birds? Which one of you can live a few years more by worrying about it?

And why worry about clothes? Look how the wild flowers grow: they do not work or make clothes for themselves. But I tell you that not even Solomon, as rich as he was, had clothes as beautiful as one of these flowers. It is God who clothes the wild grass—grass that is here today, gone tomorrow, burned up in the oven. Will he not be all the more sure to clothe you? How little is your faith! So do not start worrying: "Where will my food come from? or my drink? or my clothes?" (These are the things the heathen are always after.) Your Father in heaven knows that you need all these things. Instead, give first place to his Kingdom and to what he requires, and he will provide you with all these other things. So do not worry about tomorrow; it will have enough worries of its own.

—MATTHEW 6:25–34 (TEV)

To have faith is to be sure of the things we hope for, to be certain of the things we cannot see. . . . It was faith that made Abraham obey when God called him, and go out to a country which God had promised to give him. He left his own country without knowing where he was going. By faith he lived in the country God had promised him, as though he were in a foreign country. He lived in tents with Isaac and Jacob who had received the same promise from God. . . . They . . . admitted openly that they were foreigners and refugees on earth. . . . And so God is not ashamed to have them call him their God, for he has prepared a city for them.

—HEBREWS 11:1, 8–9, 13, 16 (TEV)

Yahweh, my heart has no lofty ambitions,
    my eyes do not look too high.
I am not concerned with great affairs
    or marvels beyond my scope.
Enough for me to keep my soul tranquil and quiet
    like a child in its mother's arms,
as content as a child that has been weaned.

Israel, rely on Yahweh,
    now and for always!

—PSALM 131 (JB)

Kishan Babu
I admire you!
How can you keep hoping
    when things are hopeless?
How can you keep going
    when you've got no place to go?
How can you still have
    faith in the future?

You know that
living
is more than
having

You're tough
tenacious
you hang in there
you won't give up
If that's what
faith is all about
you've got it

Lord,
teach me that
having
is less than
living
free me from
the desire to be a big deal
reduce my wants
to the size of my needs
give me
the gift of
simplicity

How I worry
when things are out of my
control
and I am at the mercy of
events or other people
teach me
the patience of
unfulfilled hopes
help me
always to look forward
never to give up
strengthen me
to do what I can
today
and to trust You for
tomorrow

Alone

A young man crippled by polio dragged and clawed his way to the aid of a little boy whom he rescued from strangling by his jacket near the top of a backyard gym set, doctors at Omaha Children's Hospital said Saturday.

The physician credited Arlan Greve, 26, with saving the life of Dean Alexis Zerbe, 3, son of Mr. and Mrs. Mason Zerbe and grandson of veteran top-level U. S. diplomat, U. Alexis Johnson, now ambassador to Japan.

Leaning on a pair of crutches, Greve looked out the back window of his home Thursday and saw the motionless body of little Dean Alexis in the backyard of the Zerbe home. The Zerbe backyard borders on the Greve backyard.

Greve, a laboratory technician at Nebraska Methodist Hospital here, yelled for help but got no response. He made his way through the yard to a wire fence which separates the Greve and Zerbe properties. The gym set was close to the fence but not close enough for Greve to reach the boy, who had turned blue from choking.

Greve, a polio victim 15 years ago, threw his crutches over the fence and then leaned backward on the fence until his weight plunged him into the Zerbe yard.

Greve clawed his way up the gym set and freed the tangled jacket hood and the boy from the set.

"I don't know how I got up or got the boy down. I usually can't do that sort of thing," Greve said.

First, he tried mouth to mouth resuscitation. But when that did not work, he switched to artificial respiration. Little Dean Alexis started breathing, but remained unconscious.

For 15 minutes Greve yelled for help. Only when he was convinced the boy's breathing was regular did he go to the

Zerbe door and summon Mrs. Zerbe. In turn, the mother called a rescue squad and other neighbors.

The boy was taken to Children's Hospital and later released.

—OMAHA, NEBRASKA, UPI

And Jacob was left alone; and a man wrestled with him until the breaking of the day. When the man saw that he did not prevail against Jacob, he touched the hollow of his thigh; and Jacob's thigh was put out of joint as he wrestled with him. Then he said, "Let me go, for the day is breaking." But Jacob said, "I will not let you go, unless you bless me." And he said to him, "What is your name?" And he said, "Jacob." Then he said, "Your name shall no more be called Jacob, but Israel, for you have striven with God and with men, and have prevailed." Then Jacob asked him, "Tell me, I pray, your name." But he said, "Why is it that you ask my name?" And there he blessed him. So Jacob called the name of the place Péniel (the face of God), saying, "For I have seen God face to face, and yet my life is preserved." The sun rose upon him as he passed Pénuel, limping because of his thigh.

—GENESIS 32:24–31 (RSV)

Filled with the Holy Spirit, Jesus left the Jordan and was led by the Spirit through the wilderness, being tempted there by the devil for forty days. During that time he ate nothing and at the end he was hungry. Then the devil said to him, "If you are the Son of God, tell this stone to turn into a loaf." But Jesus replied, "Scripture says: Man does not live on bread alone." Then leading him to a height, the devil showed him in a moment of time all the kingdoms of the world and said to him, "I will give you all this power and the glory of these kingdoms, for it has been committed to me and I give it to anyone I choose. Worship me, then, and it shall all be yours." But Jesus answered him, "Scripture says:

> You must worship the Lord your God,
> and serve him alone."

Then he led him to Jerusalem and made him stand on the parapet of the Temple. "If you are the Son of God," he said to him, "throw yourself down from here, for scripture says:

He will put his angels in charge of you
to guard you,

and again,

They will hold you up in their hands
in case you hurt your foot against a stone."

But Jesus answered him, "It has been said:

You must not put the Lord your God to the test."

Having exhausted all these ways of tempting him, the devil left him, to return at the appointed time.   —LUKE 4:1–13 (JB)

Alone

    in the night
    the wilderness
    the backyard

Alone

    no warning
    no one to help
    no escape

Alone

    struggling
    against fear
    of failure

Alone

    summoning the will
    grappling the enemy
    fighting to the death

Alone

    crawling
    wrestling
    withstanding

Alone

    giving out?
    giving up?
    giving in?

Alone

    reaching
    prevailing
    enduring

Alone

The Moment of Truth

The captain of a Dutch ocean-going tugboat guides his ships through the cold arctic terror of the Murmansk convoy run in the Second World War. Enemy planes and submarines decimate and scatter the convoy. Finally, the captain's ship explodes and what's left of the crew pushes off into a lifeboat. They hear a man in the water screaming for help, and when they pull him in, discover he is a young German survivor of a submarine hit by a depth charge. One of the men rises up to kill the German boy, but the captain intervenes, as a Nazi plane roars in to machine-gun the lifeboat.

I don't know what made me do it, but something in the German boy's horror at seeing the plane swoop down on him, to snuff out his pathetic little light in the vastness of the sea, made me want to protect him from the ultimate truth. I pulled him down and threw myself on top of him. . . . I lay on top of the trembling boy for what seemed an eternity. I smelled the reek of oil on his face. I felt the small warmth of his panting breath on my cheek, I heard his voice whimper close to my ear, 'Mutti, mutti, mutti.' As the plane came screaming down, I put my hand under his head and pressed his face into my shoulder to prevent his seeing the firing squad at the moment of our execution. As I lay there, pressing his head against me, it was as if, at the very last moment I had finally touched upon the sense of life, the meaning of it all, the essence of my existence. I had a feeling of such peace, such understanding, such serenity, that it came as an anti-climax, almost as a disappointment when the world fell silent, the roar of death drew away and I realized that I would have to go on living. I lifted my head and looked around me and saw men wake up amidst the chaos of clothing and blankets and stores and bodies and oars. . . . We were picked up toward nightfall: seven men, a boy and a dog, all that was left of Holland's glory.

—JAN DE HARTOG

When Elisha came into the house, he saw the child lying dead on his bed. So he went in and shut the door upon the two of them, and prayed to the Lord. Then he went up and lay upon the child, putting his mouth upon his mouth, his eyes upon his eyes, and his hands upon his hands; and as he stretched himself upon him, the flesh of the child became warm. . . . —II KINGS 4:32–34 (JB)

One of the criminals hanging there abused him. "Are you not the Christ?" he said. "Save yourself and us as well." But the other spoke up and rebuked him. "Have you no fear of God at all?" he said. "You got the same sentence as he did, but in our case we deserved it: we are paying for what we did. But this man has done nothing wrong. Jesus," he said, "remember me when you come into your kingdom." "Indeed, I promise you," he replied, "today you will be with me in paradise." —LUKE 23:39–43 (JB)

"Be compassionate as your Father is compassionate. Do not judge, and you will not be judged yourselves; do not condemn, and you will not be condemned yourselves; grant pardon, and you will be pardoned. Give, and there will be gifts for you: a full measure, pressed down, shaken together, and running over, will be poured into your lap; because the amount you measure out is the amount you will be given back." —LUKE 6:36–38 (JB)

there are many
moments of truth
  before the very last moment
moments when
  truth becomes flesh
  to me
  in some one

being in touch with some one
  feeling warmth
  hearing breathing
  smelling
makes the meaning
human
here and now
together

together in
  danger
  death
  love
  grief
physically together
there is a body wisdom
we cannot do without

we touch upon
the sense of life when
we touch upon
each other

Who is pressing upon me, Lord?

What is
the ultimate truth
            Death?
Or is it
      protecting another
      in the moment of our danger
      comforting another
      in the moment of our desolation
                              Life?

"You Don't Have a Daddy"

It was on a Thursday, the day before the Negro payday. The eagle always flew on Friday. The teacher was asking each student how much his father would give to the Community Chest. On Friday night, each kid would get the money from his father, and on Monday he would bring it to the school. I decided I was going to buy me a Daddy right then. I had money in my pocket from shining shoes and selling papers, and whatever Helene Tucker pledged for her Daddy I was going to top it. And I'd hand the money right in. I wasn't going to wait until Monday to buy me a Daddy.

I was shaking, scared to death. The teacher opened her book and started calling out names alphabetically.

"Helene Tucker?"

"My Daddy said he'd give two dollars and fifty cents."

"That's very nice, Helene. Very, very nice, indeed."

That made me feel pretty good. It wouldn't take too much to top that. I had almost three dollars in dimes and quarters in my pocket. I stuck my hand in my pocket and held onto the money, waiting for her to call my name. But the teacher closed her book after she called everybody else in the class.

I stood up and raised my hand.

"What is it now?"

"You forgot me."

She turned toward the blackboard. "I don't have time to be playing with you, Richard."

"My Daddy said he'd . . ."

"Sit down, Richard, you're disturbing the class."

"My Daddy said he'd give . . . fifteen dollars."

She turned around and looked mad. "We are collecting this money for you and your kind, Richard Gregory. If your Daddy can give fifteen dollars you have no business being on relief."

"I got it right now, I got it right now, my Daddy gave it to me to turn in today, my Daddy said . . ."

"And furthermore," she said, looking right at me, her nostrils getting big and her lips getting thin and her eyes opening wide, "we know you don't have a Daddy."

Helene Tucker turned around, her eyes full of tears. She felt sorry for me. Then I couldn't see her too well because I was crying, too.

"Sit down, Richard."

And I always thought the teacher kind of liked me. She always picked me to wash the blackboard on Friday, after school. That was a big thrill, it made me feel important. If I didn't wash it, come Monday the school might not function right.

"Where are you going, Richard?"

I walked out of school that day, and for a long time I didn't go back very often. There was shame there.

—DICK GREGORY

When Esau heard the words of his father, he cried out with an exceedingly great and bitter cry, and said to his father, "Bless me, even me also, O my father!" But he said, "Your brother came with guile, and he has taken away your blessing." Esau said, "Is he not rightly named Jacob? For he has supplanted me these two times. He took away my birthright; and behold, now he has taken away my blessing." Then he said, "Have you not reserved a blessing for me?" Isaac answered Esau, "Behold, I have made him your lord, and all his brothers I have given to him for servants, and with grain and wine I have sustained him. What then can I do for you, my son?" Esau said to his father, "Have you but one blessing, my father? Bless me, even me also, O my father." And Esau lifted up his voice and wept.

—GENESIS 27:34–38 (RSV)

O Lord, how long shall I cry for help,
    and thou wilt not hear?
Or cry to thee, "Violence!"
    and thou wilt not save?
Why dost thou make me see wrongs
    and look upon trouble?
Destruction and violence are before me;
    strife and contention arise.
So the law is slacked
    and justice never goes forth.
For the wicked surround the righteous,
    so justice goes forth perverted.

—HABAKKUK 1:2–4 (RSV)

The word of Yahweh was addressed to me, saying,
    "Before I formed you in the womb I knew you;
    before you came to birth I consecrated you;
    I have appointed you as a prophet to the nations."
I said, "Ah, Lord Yahweh; look, I do not know how to speak:
I am a child!"
    But Yahweh replied,
    "Do not say, 'I am a child.'
    Go now to those to whom I send you
    and say whatever I command you.
    Do not be afraid of them,
    for I am with you to protect you—
    it is Yahweh who speaks!"
Then Yahweh put out his hand and touched my mouth and
said to me:
    "There! I am putting my words into your mouth.
    Look, today I am setting you
    over nations and over kingdoms,
    to tear up and to knock down,
    to destroy and to overthrow,
    to build and to plant."

"The harvest is over, summer at an end,
and we have not been saved!"
The wound of the daughter of my people wounds me too,
all looks dark to me, terror grips me.
Is there not balm in Gilead any more?
Is there no doctor there?
Then why does it make no progress,
this cure of the daughter of my people?

—JEREMIAH 1:4–10; 8:20–22 (JB)

The wound of my brother blacks
wounds me too
Is there no compassion in America anymore?
    no outrage at the mutilation of a child's spirit?
    no urgency to cure the shaming-shameful wound?

White America
prefers her
black prophets
dead
like Martin Luther King, Jr.
We admire them only
postmortem

O young black prophets!
Speak judgment
to us who neither
fear God
nor care for man.
O young innocent Richards!
twice robbed of
birthright and
blessing

twice shamed:
    violence to your bodies
    violence to your spirits
seize back
your stolen birthright
demand
your stolen blessing
cry "Violence" to the Lord!

Who's responsible for riots?
the robbed or the robbers?
the oppressed or the oppressors?

Heal the wound of Your people, O Lord
From judgment
bring forth justice;
from justice
reconciliation

Dear Mr. Grady

C.R., age seventeen, wrote these letters from New Hampton, a state training school, to Ed Grady, his former teacher at Youth House.

April 4

Dear Mr. Grady,

How are you and the family doing? Just fine I hope. As for myself, I'm fine.

I received your letter today and was very happy to hear from you. Just to know someone cared made me feel like a real person. I had given up all man kind, and was going into a world of my own.

I haven't yet to hear from my people. Mr. Grady, I'm really hurt! This morning when they said I had mail, I felt good. Then when I read your deep letter, I felt like crying. I know someone in my family had a couple of seconds to put hello on some paper and send it off. I've been here going on two months now. But getting back to your letter, it was very touching. I don't know what to say. You're the only one who stuck with me. You're like a father to me. Mr. Grady, all the things you have done for me, I don't know how to thank you.

I shouldn't be telling you my personal problems, but you're the only one I can express my feeling to. I hope you don't mind.

By the way, I would appreciate that shirt, size 18. I been wearing the same close since I been here, and I'd like to have a diary, in this way, I can keep a record of myself, and little things I say and do. (you know) I've been thinking and writing a book on my life. I wonder what would become of it, how many pages would I get?

99

Dear Mr. Grady,

I haven't yet to hear nor see my parents. Why I don't know. I'm sure it's not a money problem, because my parents both work, and my mother get's a little help from the city, which we aren't doing to bad for a family of sixteen kids. They sent my sister to school in texas just a few months ago. My older brothers and sisters work. I have a sister that workd in the post off.

Mr. Grady, do you know how I feel? Theres no reason for them to treat me this way. I'm human too. I understand you have kids to take care of and you can't play the part of my real father. Not saying I've gave you up. But don't you think it's wrong for me to look on you for my personal needs. You're the only one I can really express my feelings to. I've lost my girl friend. She gave me up! I mean, I have a child by this woman and if I lost her, I've lost all hope and dreams of ever becoming anything. I had my life planed out just swell. I was going all the way in drafting. Now I don't even care to go to class. Before I couldn't wait for the next day so I could eat up everyting the man was teaching.

But now look at me, a bum, and nothing but my close are so dirty it's funny. I can beat dust out of them.

I just wrote my mother a six page letter begging her to bring my close. I would have wrote you sooner, but I had to wait until I could get a stamp, and the only reason I got that was, my friend had a visit and was nice enough to give me two.

So I'll change the subject for now. I don't like talking about it at times, because it makes me feel real bad.

So I'm very thankful for everything. What would I do without you, Mr. Grady? Whom could I write to when I write or think about you, my mind is put to ease.

So I hope I havent upset you or put you to thinking of me because I know you have more to do.

So until the next letter is posted, I'm signing out.

Your second son,
C.R.

To Yahweh, my cry! I plead.
To Yahweh, my cry, I entreat.
I pour out my supplications,
I unfold all my troubles;
my spirit fails me,
but you, you know my path.

On the path I follow
they have concealed a trap.
Look on my right and see,
there is no one to befriend me.
All help is denied me,
no one cares about me.

I invoke you, Yahweh,
I affirm that you are my refuge,
my heritage in the land of the living.
Listen to my cries for help,
I can hardly be crushed lower.

—PSALM 142 (JB)

Yahweh, hear my voice as I cry!
   Pity me! Answer me!

Do not repulse your servant in anger;
   you are my help.
Never leave me, never desert me,
   God, my saviour!
If my father and mother desert me,
   Yahweh will care for me still.

—PSALM 27:7–14 (JB)

A man had two sons. The younger said to his father, "Father, let me have the share of the estate that would come to me." So the father divided the property between them. A few days later, the younger son got together everything he had and left for a distant country where he squandered his money on a life of debauchery.

When he had spent it all, that country experienced a severe famine, and now he began to feel the pinch, so he hired himself out to one of the local inhabitants who put him on his farm to feed the pigs. And he would willingly have filled his belly with the husks the pigs were eating but no one offered him anything. Then he came to his senses and said, "How many of my father's paid servants have more food than they want, and here I am dying of hunger! I will leave this place and go to my father and say: Father, I have sinned against heaven and against you; I no longer deserve to be called your son; treat me as one of your paid servants." So he left the place and went back to his father.

While he was still a long way off, his father saw him and was moved with pity. He ran to the boy, clasped him in his arms and kissed him tenderly. Then his son said, "Father, I have sinned against heaven and against you. I no longer deserve to be called your son." But the father said to his servants, "Quick! Bring out the best robe and put it on him; put a ring on his finger and sandals on his feet. Bring the calf we have been fattening, and kill it; we are going to have a feast, a celebration, because this son of mine was dead and has come back to life; he was lost and is found." And they began to celebrate. —LUKE 15:11–24 (JB)

Not to have a letter
to be sentenced to
silence
is to be cut off
from the land of the living
not remembered
without a name
nameless

Not to have your own clothes
to be shorn of part
of yourself
is to be left
without protection
naked

To lose a friend
is to have your
confidence
broken
your joy
crushed
your hopes
dashed
is to be a bum
in the eyes of the world
and worse
in your own eyes
a nobody

To make a diary
is to be sure
you exist
every day
to record
for all to see,
but especially
for you to see
   this is what I did
   this is what I said
   this is who I am
I am for real
I have a name
I have my own clothes
I am somebody

God,
it helps
to pour out myself
to You
and to know
that whatever happens
and
whoever forgets me
You will remember
me

The Spirit of the Bayonet

1 July 1969

Dear Mom and Dad:

In many respects the Army is not as bad as I expected, but overall, it's still the worst thing that ever happened to me. The thing that makes me angriest is the constant harassment for no apparent reason. Actually there is a reason for it, but when you figure it out you wish there weren't one at all—they want us to get angry enough to kill. It works—one fellow I know is a C.O. [conscientious objector] and he gets harassed more than anyone. They give him extra guard duty, trash details, yard details—anything that comes up—just because of his political beliefs.

I got really depressed this afternoon when they issued us our rifles. An M-14 is a pretty useless weapon for hunting or target shooting—the only thing it can be used really effectively and efficaciously for is to kill a human being. I still don't feel like a killer—I guess I will in 8 weeks, but I don't like it. If it were not against the law to express political opinions in this country, I'd tell ——— to go to Canada.

8 July 1969

The worst thing so far has been bayonet drill. Whenever they ask us, "What is the spirit of the bayonet?" we have to yell at the top of our lungs, "To kill! to kill! To kill without mercy!" "And what does that make you?" "Killers!" "What kind of killers?" "Merciless killers!"

When is it that you're planning on coming? I'm only allowed visitors on weekends and then only if everybody in the platoon did a good job of learning how to move without thinking and how to kill without mercy during the week. It's kind of funny how responsibility changes someone. If I weren't married and hoping to provide my wife a decent home and to have a couple of kids in a few years, I'd be in jail right now for total refusal to obey any and all lawful orders. There's a bunch of us here who don't shout "To kill!" any more; instead we shout "To build!" and instead of "Merciless killer!" we shout "Harmless Feller!" Our greeting is the raised two fingers of the Peace movement.

Love,

B.

Letter from the boy's father to a minister

Enclosed is a copy of a letter which says a few things about the problems he is facing now, and raises some questions about our national morality.

How do you rationalize the "spirit of the bayonet" with the Holy Spirit? I know he would have to be "brainwashed" to become a soldier, but how do you get rid of the scars—how does he return to his former "un-washed" condition?

In his silent resistance I see some hope.

All of this seems to be the essence of confusion. How do love, bayonet, gas, and all the rest get mixed together? What kind of games are we playing? The tragedy is—the average God-fearing church-going Christian can't see the irony of it all. . . . What do I do about it?

Sincerely,

———

Moses said to the people, "Some of you must take arms to wage Yahweh's campaign against Midian, to carry out the vengeance of Yahweh on Midian." . . .

They waged the campaign against Midian, as Yahweh had ordered Moses, and they put every male to death. And further, they killed the kings of Midian. . . . they also put Balaam son of Beor to the sword. The son of Israel took Midianite women captive with their young children, and plundered all their cattle, all their flocks and all their goods. They set fire to the towns where they lived and all their encampments. Then, taking all their booty, all that they had captured, man and beast, they took the captives, spoil, and booty to Moses. . . . Moses . . . went out of the camp to meet them. Moses was enraged with the commanders of the army . . . who had come back from this military expedition. He said, "Why have you spared the life of all the women? These were the very ones who, on Balaam's advice, perverted the sons of Israel and made them renounce Yahweh in the affair at Peor: hence the plague which struck the community of Israel. So kill all the male children. Kill also all the women who have slept with a man. Spare the lives only of the young girls who have not slept with a man, and take them for yourselves . . ."

—NUMBERS 31:3, 7–18 (JB)

What the Spirit brings is very different: love, joy, peace, patience, kindness, goodness, trustfulness, gentleness and self-control. There can be no law against things like that, of course. . . . Since the Spirit is our life, let us be directed by the Spirit. —GALATIANS 5:22, 25 (JB)

You have learnt how it was said to our ancestors:
You must not kill . . .
But I say this to you: any one who is angry with his brother will answer for it. . . .

You have learnt how it was said:
You must love your neighbor and hate your enemy.
But I say this to you:
love your enemies . . .   —MATTHEW 5:21–22, 43–44 (JB)

How do you rationalize
"the spirit of the bayonet" with
the Holy Spirit?
I don't know
I don't think
you can

Is God
a God of war?
No!
That's blasphemy!
Is God
"on our side"?
No!
That's blasphemy!

"Kill a Commie for Christ"
How can a Christian
kill?

How can I love
my enemy by
killing him?

How can I take
Jesus' teaching seriously
without becoming a
pacifist?

But I am not a
pacifist
though I respect greatly
those who are
I would fight—
even kill?—
to protect my family
or defend my country
How can a Christian
kill?

I don't want
my son
to learn to be a
killer
the scars remain

Are there
just wars?
Whose justice?
Who decides?

Lord, I am confused,
what can I do?

Prey And Predator Alike

One fortunate troop [of baboons] . . . slept in an almost inaccessible cave 500 feet high on a sheerest cliff. There was a way to the cave, a ledge half a mile long and in places only six inches wide that overhung like the cave itself a fall as fatal for baboons as for baboon enemies. In the hour before midnight the ledge would be crowded with the troop seeking safety. Marais would watch, and marvel at the orderly movement. Caution for once stilled baboon chatter. Adult males led, then childless females, then females to whose backs and bellies clung infants. Marais noted that peril might still the baboon voice, but not the play of baboon young. At the most dangerous corners children could not resist the temptation of pulling the convenient tails of their neighbors. But at last the cave would fill, and the ledge would clear. Night would fall, and death would move on unheard feet through wood and bush and clearing. Cold stars, brutal in their impassivity, would make of the sky an emptier thing. But at least one society of animals was safe, and would sleep in peace.

Other troops in the Waterberg, such as Marais' own, possessed no strongholds of comparable strength. Yet to all, whatever their insecurity, night brought the same spectre. . . .

It was still dusk. The troop had only just returned from the feeding grounds and had barely time to reach its scattered sleeping places in the high-piled rocks behind the fig tree. Now it shrilled its terror. And Marais could see the leopard. It appeared from the bush and took its insolent time. So vulnerable were the baboons that the leopard seemed to recognize no need for hurry. He crouched just below a little jutting cliff observing his prey and the problems of the terrain. And Marais saw two male baboons edging along the cliff above him.

The two males moved cautiously. The leopard, if he saw them, ignored them. His attention was fixed on the swarming, screeching, defenseless horde scrambling among the rocks. Then the two males dropped. They dropped on him from a height of 12 feet. One bit at the leopard's spine. The other struck at this throat while clinging to his neck from below. In an instant the leopard disemboweled with his hind claws the baboon hanging to his neck and caught in his jaws the baboon on his back. But it was too late. The dying, disemboweled baboon had hung on just long enough and had reached the leopard's jugular vein with his canines.

Marais watched while movement stilled beneath the little jutting cliff. Night fell. Death, hidden from all but the impartial stars, enveloped prey and predator alike. And in the hollow places in the rocky, looming krans a society of animals settled down to sleep.

—ROBERT ARDREY

From your palace you water the uplands
until the ground has had all that your heavens have to offer;
you make fresh grass grow for cattle
and those plants made use of by man,
for them to get food from the soil:
wine to make them cheerful,
oil to make them happy
and bread to make them strong.

The trees of Yahweh get rain enough,
those cedars of Lebanon he planted;
here the little birds build their nest
and, on the highest branches, the stork has its home.
For the wild goats there are the mountains,
in the crags rock-badgers hide.

You made the moon to tell the seasons,
the sun knows when to set:

you bring darkness on, night falls,
all the forest animals come out:
savage lions roaring for their prey,
claiming their food from God.

—PSALM 104:13–21 (JB)

The wolf shall dwell with the lamb, and the leopard shall lie down with the kid, and the calf and the lion and the fatling together, and a little child shall lead them. The cow and the bear shall feed; their young shall lie down together; and the lion shall eat straw like the ox. The sucking child shall play over the hole of the asp, and the weaned child shall put his hand on the adder's den. They shall not hurt or destroy in all my holy mountain; for the earth shall be full of the knowledge of the Lord as the waters cover the sea. —ISAIAH 11:6–9 (RSV)

Two baboons
and a leopard
lying down together
in death
to be killed
while killing

There's a baboon in me
a hidden hero
a tragic clown
a crying comic
with a capacity
for sacrifice

There's a leopard in me
a proud savage
on the make
a ruthless beast
with a capacity
for cruelty

Who am I?
One or the other
or both?
Can a baboon
and a leopard
lie down together
and live?

The Public Enemy

It is a beautiful May morning. Sunlight streams through the window. Birds chatter, the heady odor of wisteria floats on the exhaust fumes. Suddenly, for no logical reason at all, you feel good.

Alarms sound throughout the city, warning the populace that someone has awakened feeling good and will soon be moving through the streets, corridors, fluorescent cells. A smiler is within the gates. Orders are dispatched along the extrasensory communications net that binds the city's defense system.

"Report of a man feeling good at Elm and Main. Use extreme caution. May be happy."

It is a terrible situation, but exhilarating for all that. Soon the whole city will be after you. Is it best to give up immediately? That would be the easy way normally, but there is no getting around the fact that you feel good, really good, and if you are cunning and brave maybe you can take a few down smiling with you before you are zapped.

"Feeling good, aren't you," says rather than asks the woman making breakfast. She is hooked in the warning net, too.

"Can you ever forgive me, Emma? I didn't mean to feel good. I just woke up this morning and the sunlight was streaming in and there was the smell of wisteria on the exhaust fumes. . . ."

"You have no right to feel good. Don't you realize you can't just wake up feeling good whenever there's a little sunlight? If you'd think about my miseries once in a while instead of your own selfish pleasures, you wouldn't be in this predicament."

As she natters on you realize that she is stalling for time until the psychiatrist can get there. Over the back fence you go and down the alley, smiling at dogs.

At the bus stop a familiar face (Tom's) registers surprise and hostility. "You've got your nerve!"

"I can't help myself, Tom."

"How can you feel good when you think about all the poor people there are?"

"The sunlight was so lovely . . ."

"You're a disgrace to your class."

"I hate myself for not being poor, Tom, but I just can't stop feeling good in spite of it."

At the office it is even worse. A picket line of idealists is tearing up the cobblestones. "Are you the man who feels good?" their leader demands.

"Me? You must be insane. How could anyone even think of feeling good when he contemplates his own personal responsibility for police brutality, college presidents, Lawrence Welk, Christopher Columbus, the Crusades, old Pharaoh, Kaiser Wilhelm, Mussolini, Dow Chemical and the population explosion?"

It is a close thing but the chief idealist buys it. "Okay," he grunts. "Have a dyspeptic day."

It makes you feel really good to put one over on an idealist. In fact, it makes you feel so good that you feel bad about it. What are you, anyhow? Some kind of a social fink? Everyone else can wake up with the sunshine streaming through the window without letting it make him feel good.

In the office Miss Pansky is near tears. "You! Of all people!" she cries. "Just last night I was telling my roommate what a beautiful sense of guilt you had."

"I didn't mean to feel good, Miss Pansky. The sunlight—"

" 'He'll never let himself quit despairing for a minute,' I told my roommate. 'Not as long as there are nuclear weapons and unsafe autos and bad boys and teams that lose at football.' "

"Would it help if I told you honestly that feeling good makes me feel like an absolute rat?"

"Don't go for your smile!"

It is the misery squad. The jig is up. They carry tear gas.

Now, you must be reclaimed for society. The psychiatrist is so understanding. "Now, when you thought you were feeling good this morning, what was it you were really feeling?" And so on. In no time at all he proves that it is utterly impossible for you to have felt good at any time in your life or ever to feel good at any time in the future.

How sweet is the absolution. How understanding is the entire society which you have nearly destroyed. You have learned your lesson. Misery no longer loves company. Nowadays it insists upon it.

—RUSSELL BAKER

When Moses came down from Mount Sinai, with the two tables of the testimony in his hand as he came down from the mountain, Moses did not know that the skin of his face shone because he had been talking with God. And when Aaron and all the people of Israel saw Moses, behold, the skin of his face shone, and they were afraid to come near him. But Moses called to them; and Aaron and all the leaders of the congregation returned to him, and Moses talked with them. And afterward all the people of Israel came near, and he gave them in commandment all that the Lord had spoken with him in Mount Sinai. And when Moses had finished speaking with them, he put a veil on his face; but whenever Moses went in before the Lord to speak with him, he took the veil off, until he came out; and when he came out, and told the people of Israel what he was commanded, the people of Israel saw the face of Moses, that the skin of Moses' face shone; and Moses would put the veil upon his face again, until he went in to speak with him.

—EXODUS 34:29–35 (RSV)

As the members of the Council listened to Stephen they became furious and ground their teeth at him in anger. But Stephen, full of the Holy Spirit, looked up to heaven and saw God's glory, and Jesus standing at the right side of God. "Look!" he said. "I see heaven opened and the Son of Man standing at the right side of God!" With a loud cry they stopped up their ears, and all rushed together at him at once. They threw him out of the city and stoned him. The witnesses left their cloaks in charge of a young man named Saul. They

113

kept on stoning Stephen as he called on the Lord, "Lord Jesus, receive my spirit!" He knelt down and cried in a loud voice, "Lord! Do not remember this sin against them!" He said this and died.   —ACTS 7:54–60 (TEV)

. . . Where the Spirit of the Lord is, there is freedom. And we, with our unveiled faces reflecting like mirrors the brightness of the Lord, all grow brighter and brighter as we are turned into the image that we reflect; this is the work of the Lord who is Spirit. . . . For it is not ourselves that we preach: we preach Jesus Christ as Lord, and ourselves as your servants for Jesus' sake. The God who said, "Out of darkness the light shall shine!" is the same God who made his light shine in our hearts, to bring us the light of the knowledge of God's glory, shining in the face of Christ.

—II CORINTHIANS 3:17–18 (JB); 4:5–6 (TEV)

Nailed again!
Here I am
    leading the misery squad
    making people feel guilty
    dispensing tear gas all over the place

Lord,
give me a little laughing gas
please?
or at least some smiling gas
Wouldn't that be a gas!
    Me!
    a smiler within the gates
    a whistler within the walls

Why do I try to
poke holes in someone else's
happiness?

Am I jealous of
happy people?
Do I feel judged
by another's joy?
Or guilty about
happiness:
   mine or anybody else's?

Is there a difference between
being careless
of human misery
and
being carefree
in the midst of it
caring
but
free of care?

There's something
   holy about happiness
   healing about smiling

I would like to be
   a smiler within the gates
   a whistler within the walls

Gift from a Hair Dryer

As she scrambles out of the Saturday night bath and shampoo, dripping dark green footprints on the light green mat, you throw a towel around her head and rub vigorously as she jumps up and down.

"Mommy, I've got goose pimples!"

"Stand still," you say, handing her another towel. "Dry yourself while I rub your hair."

Five minutes later she is pink pajamaed, clean-toothed and sitting crosslegged on her bed, damp hair going in all directions. She resembles nothing so much as a newly hatched chicken. You perch beside her and plug in the hand-operated hair dryer, pointing it at the nape of her neck.

"It's nice and warm," she says, reaching for a book. "I'll read you a story while it dries."

"Good," you say, combing from south to north on the back of her head and directing the warm air stream into the moving hair, watching it fall in layers, finely, as it sifts apart from the damp mass. A horizontal part moves upward following the comb. Over and over again—south to north, hair falling, air blowing.

" 'John and Cindy had a little dog. He was brown and white. His name was Toby.' " Second grade reading books are fascinating to second graders, and that is as it should be. You find your fascination elsewhere, in the way the light falls on the gold-brown strands.

" 'Go get the ball, Toby,' " she reads on. You are trying to decide whether she is really quite beautiful or just ordinary and beloved. Likely not beautiful. But beloved.

The comb lifts the hair, baring a pink ear scrubbed to Saturday night perfection. Something about the pink ear takes you back over the years, and you remember this same head, baby-bald as a darning egg. Then came blonde curls. Now no curls and not any special color, but clean and soft and shining, warm-laid on the side of her cheek.

" 'John and Cindy went looking for their dog.' " You are not listening.

Comb and dry, comb and dry. You half close your eyes and pick another memory out of her blowing hair. She was three that summer on Cape Cod when the strong sea wind blew the curls up from her neck just like this. You remember how she turned around and suddenly up went the bangs, baring a white forehead above sun-pink nose and cheeks. You remember the unbelievable quantity of sand she carried home on her scalp that day to be brushed out on the cottage floor. How little she was then! And now seven. Seven!

The air current swings her hair suddenly to one side, and she is five again, skipping off to her first day at kindergarten, the breezes undoing all the work of a careful comb as they play through her hair, swaying it like this in rhythm to her skipping. The cadence of her merry gait captures you completely even now, two years later.

She coughs you back into Saturday night on the edge of her bed and goes on reading. " 'The children asked the grocery store man if he had seen Toby.' "

"Turn around now," you say. "Let's do the other side. It's dry over here." Yes, she is beautiful. You have decided it, and that is that.

Comb and dry, comb and dry. "Soon I won't be able to do this any more," you say to yourself, knowing that the little straight bob must inevitably yield to grownup coiffures and ugly curlers. What will she be like at fourteen? Where will her hair be blowing then? And sixteen and eighteen—you suppose boys will love to watch her hair blow as you do now. And some of them will feel it on their faces, and one of them will marry her, and her hair will be perfect under the veil, and there will be her hair spread out on his pillow . . . oh, you hate him a little and wonder where he is at this moment and whether he'll be good to her. . . . they will grow old together. . . . this gold-brown hair will be gray, and you will be gone, and then she will be gone. . . . this very hair that now your fingers smooth. . . .

All the tears of the world swim for a second in your eyes as you snatch the plug out of the socket suddenly and gather her into your arms, burying your face in the warm hair as if you could somehow seal this moment against all time.

"Hey, don't you know we're just at the end of the story?" she asks, surprised by your embrace.

"Yes, honey. Of course."

"I peeked ahead. They find their dog. It's a happy story."

"I knew it would be."

She reads the last page. You sing an evening song together, exchange kisses on each other's noses, turn out the light and go downstairs to finish the ironing as if nothing bittersweet and wonderful had happened.

—MARY JEAN IRION

For everything there is a season, and a time for every matter under heaven:
a time to be born, and a time to die;
a time to plant, and a time to pluck up what is planted . . .
a time to weep, and a time to laugh;
a time to mourn, and a time to dance;
a time to embrace, and a time to refrain from embracing . . .
a time to seek, and a time to lose;
a time to keep, and a time to cast away. . . .
He has made everything beautiful in its time.

—ECCLESIASTES 3:1–6, 11 (RSV)

Yet it was I who taught Ephraim to walk,
I took them up in my arms;
but they did not know that I healed them.
I led them with cords of compassion,
with bands of love,
and I became to them as one
who eases the yoke on their jaws,
and I bent down to them and fed them.

—HOSEA 11:3–4 (RSV)

And they went with haste, and found Mary and Joseph, and the babe lying in a manger. And when they saw it they made known the saying which had been told them concerning this child; and all who heard it wondered at what the shepherds told them. But Mary kept all these things, pondering them in her heart.

—LUKE 2:16–19 (RSV)

Bittersweet is beautiful
in its time
                    is love lost
        or remembered
                    is wanting
            this time
            for all time
                as time goes by
            with time on my hands
Are my times in Your hand,
O Lord?

Beautiful is bittersweet
in its time
                    is wanting to
kill time
            so as to save time
                and have time
            to hold my beloved
            against the time
                as time marches on
            with my beloved in my arms
Is my beloved in Your arms,
O Lord?

        O bitter is the beauty
            when tender is the time!

Both Master And Clay

Now he empties the big hunks of clay, plunks down his vision. Shells bite. Rocks bruise. The ancient Ordovician life resists him. The clay's not putty in his hands. He sets himself to master the clay. This is not easy. He lifts it up above his head and whacks it down. The thump and bang of earth goes on and on. If the earth's not welded, the pot's going to split and crumble. The hateful lessons of life begin to emerge in all their native starkness.

But at last his fingers feel they've got the stuff together, for the best of it, got the best out of it, and on to the throwing head it goes. Now the vision returns. Now's the time to think of life . . . forget what it's been, forget what it looks like without its leaves. Here's another chance. Here's this big homely clump of greasy grey clay, the old bones crunched up, shells fragmented, millions of years gone into the making, old wars forgotten, old feuds mastered, all the eating and being eaten, the winds gone over, the seas dried up. And here we are.

First you have to have a vision, you have to see what you want out of this unpromising bulk of old ancestral storms. It's there; it's been done—the miracle's no cheat. Then you have to get this lump exactly centered on the wheel; that's been done, that's possible too. Man's a discriminating beast as well as a strong one—and then—oh, then—the turning and whirling begins. Get both hands around this clay, this life, around and around, and it starts to stretch and grow, and, as it stretches you have to know its "innate tensile strength," a master potter said—you have to know *this* clay's capacity to stretch, its exact point, beyond which, below which, it's not that which it could have been, the realization of its whole capacity. . . .

The uncouth slippery lump athwart the wheel (or head) begins to rise, spiraling around and rising dizzily. The potter gouges down with thumbs inside, the hole begins to grow, the hollow heart enlarges. Hold on! The clay's still got some life of its own—it starts to weave and loop, lean outward, its eye on freedom—whole bowls have found escape, shot off the whirling head, found the farthest corner of the room, gone back to blob. My heart's been with them, but it's no use. Scoop yourself up—man's both master and clay of his own life. Dry off the wheel head. Plunk down, center the clay again. Grab the stuff with both hands and here we go again (in the end we'll thank those sharp thumbs in our eyes, won't we, O beautiful form, O wide and graceful flare, O vessel of the Lord). This is better than lying in the corner covered with dust cats, a mystery to night mice. Yes, this is a far, far better thing we be. . . .

Then there's the miracle of firing that turns this grey greasy clay into a rough, red brown that sparks with life. The miracle of glaze that shuts its pores. Makes rainbows. And the miracle of shape from shapeless clay. The potter's world is an extraordinary one. It's man's history and man himself. Grog, slip and slurry, flock, rib and wedge, center and master. And in the end, burned earth, *keramos*, that which is rock and can never be softened or worked again. But can be broken.

—JOSEPHINE JOHNSON

The word that was addressed to Jeremiah by Yahweh, "Get up and make your way down to the potter's house; there I shall let you hear what I have to say." So I went down to the potter's house; and there he was, working at the wheel. And whenever the vessel he was making came out wrong, as happens with the clay handled by potters, he would start afresh and work it into another vessel, as potters do. Then this word of Yahweh was addressed to me, "House of Israel, can not I do to you what this potter does?—it is Yahweh who speaks. Yes, as the clay is in the potter's hand, so you are in mine."

—JEREMIAH 18:1–6 (JB)

Yet we who have this spiritual treasure are like common clay pots to show that the supreme power belongs to God, not to us. We are often troubled, but not crushed; sometimes in doubt, but never in despair; there are many enemies, but we are never without a friend; and though badly hurt at times, we are not destroyed. . . . Even though our outward nature is decaying, our inward nature is being made new day after day. And this small and temporary trouble we suffer will bring us a tremendous and eternal glory, much greater than the trouble. For we fix our attention, not on the things that are seen, but on things that are unseen. What can be seen lasts only for a time; but what cannot be seen lasts for ever.

—II CORINTHIANS 4:7–9, 16–18 (TEV)

The Lord Jesus on the night when he was betrayed took bread, and when he had given thanks he broke it, and said, "This is my body which is broken for you."

—I CORINTHIANS 11:23–24 (RSV, variant reading)

Here I am
clay
to shape
and
be shaped
to master
and be mastered

Here I am
turning
whirling
stuff of
past/future
where I come from
where I'm going
alpha
and
omega
world without end Amen

But not yet
now
still stretching
neither beyond
nor below
but
rising
yeast of God
yearning escape
in formlessness
learning freedom
in form

Miracle
of
me
in
Your hands
broken

In the Dark

But let me describe the music school. I love it here. It is the basement of a huge Baptist church. Golden collection plates rest on the table beside me. Girls in their first blush of adolesence, carrying fawn-colored flute cases and pallid folders of music, shuffle by me; their awkwardness is lovely, like the stance of a bather testing the sea. Boys and mothers arrive and leave. From all directions sounds—of pianos, oboes, clarinets —arrive like hints of another world, a world where angels fumble, pause, and begin again. . . .

My daughter is just beginning the piano. These are her first lessons, she is eight, she is eager and hopeful. Silently she sits beside me as we drive the nine miles to the town where the lessons are given; silently she sits beside me, in the dark, as we drive home. Unlike her, she does not beg for a reward of candy or a Coke, as if the lesson itself has been a meal. She only remarks—speaking dully, as if in a reflex of greed she has outgrown—that the store windows are decorated for Christmas already. I love taking her, I love waiting for her, I love driving her home through the mystery of darkness toward the certainty of supper. I do this taking and driving because today my wife visits her psychiatrist. She visits a psychiatrist because I am unfaithful to her. I do not understand the connection, but there seems to be one.

—JOHN UPDIKE

But where shall wisdom be found?
And where is the place of understanding?
"Behold, the fear of the Lord, that is wisdom;
and to depart from evil is understanding."

JOB 28:12, 28 (RSV)

Where could I go to escape your spirit?
Where could I flee from your presence?
If I climb the heavens, you are there,
there too, if I lie in Sheol.

If I flew to the point of sunrise,
or westward across the sea,
your handing would still be guiding me,
your right hand holding me.

If I asked darkness to cover me,
and light to become night around me,
that darkness would not be dark to you,
night would be as light as day.

It was you who created my inmost self,
and put me together in my mother's womb;
for all these mysteries I thank you:
for the wonder of myself, for the wonder of your works.

You know me through and through.

—PSALM 139:7–15 (JB)

The scribes and Pharisees brought a woman along who had been caught committing adultery; and making her stand there in full view of everybody, they said to Jesus, "Master, this woman was caught in the very act of committing adultery, and Moses has ordered us in the Law to condemn women like this to death by stoning. What have you to say?" They asked him this as a test, looking for something to use against him. But Jesus bent down and started writing on the ground with his finger. As they persisted with their question, he looked up and said, "If there is one of you who has not sinned, let him be the first to throw a stone at her." Then he bent down and wrote on the ground again. When they heard this they went away one by one, beginning with the eldest, until Jesus was left alone with the woman, who remained standing there. He looked up and said, "Woman, where are they? Has no one con-

demned you?" "No one, sir," she replied. "Neither do I condemn you," said Jesus, "go away, and don't sin any more."
    When Jesus spoke to the people again, he said:
    "I am the light of the world;
    anyone who follows me will not be walking in the
        dark. . . ."

—JOHN 8:3–12 (JB)

In the dark
that's where I am too
it's so easy to
see into someone else's dark
so hard to
see in my own dark

How I love being
with my daughter
in the silent companionship
of trust
together
I who am wise as a serpent
and do not understand
she who is innocent as a dove
and sees in the dark

Is it that I like the dark
and its hidden mysteries
or
am I bored with the light
and its revealed certainties

Have I lost my way
or chosen my way
Am I lost
or could I
find my way out of the dark
if I wanted to

What is it I don't understand:
my friend-enemy?
myself?
Do I want to understand
myself
or am I hiding in the dark

God, I am comforted
to know that
You know
me
Yet You don't condemn me
You could
others do
I do myself, sometimes

I seem able to defend myself
against condemnation
it's understanding that
undermines
my not understanding
till I begin to
understand

A Strange Joy

The following prayer was offered by Miss Susannah H. Wood, a graduating senior, at the Radcliffe baccalaureate service, 1968.

We pray that You will hear us as we think about our graduation, even though we have trouble using the traditional language for talking to You and though many of us no longer feel a part of a religious community.

Graduation presses the past and the future together in our minds so that we face it with mixed feelings and we do not know what to affirm.

It is especially hard for us because the events of this year have forced us to have a personal reaction to public events. We do not feel like a cool, swinging generation—we are eaten up inside by an intensity that we cannot name.

Somehow this year more than others, we have had to draw lines, to try to find an absolute right with which we could identify ourselves. First in the face of the daily killings and draft calls of the curiously undeclared Vietnam War. Then with the assassinations of Martin Luther King and Senator Kennedy.

There is a strain in all we do—a sense of "the time is now," added to what we would feel anyway as we graduate. We are grateful for what we have learned and experienced here, but we are not sure we have done the best we could. We feel we have gained a certain competence, but realize we fall far short of what we would do or be. We are excited about next year, but frightened of it at the same time.

We pray that You will help us accept the past and face the future with courage and dignity. Help us to leave our friends with love that does not depend on geography, and to face loneliness if we must with a willingness to appreciate without desire to be appreciated.

Help us to prepare a kind of renaissance in our public and private lives. Let there be born in us a strange joy, that will help us to live and to die and to remake the soul of our time.

He took his staff in his hand, picked five smooth stones from the river bed, put them in his shepherd's bag, in his pouch, and with his sling in his hand he went to meet the Philistine. The Philistine, his shield-bearer in front of him, came nearer and nearer to David; and the Philistine looked at David and what he saw filled him with scorn, because David was only a youth, a boy of fresh complexion and pleasant bearing. . . . No sooner had the Philistine started forward to confront David than David left the line of battle and ran to meet the Philistine. Putting his hand in his bag, he took out a stone and slung it and struck the Philistine on the forehead; the stone penetrated the forehead and he fell on his face to the ground. Thus David triumphed over the Philistine with a sling and a stone. . . . —I SAMUEL 17:40–42, 48–50 (JB)

From the depths I call to you, Yahweh,
Lord, listen to my cry for help!
Listen compassionately
    to my pleading!

If you never overlooked our sins, Yahweh,
Lord, could any one survive?
But you do forgive us:
    and for that we revere you.

I wait for Yahweh, my soul waits for him,
    I rely on his promise,
    my soul relies on the Lord
    more than a watchman on the coming of dawn. . . .

God, you are my God, I am seeking you,
my soul is thirsting for you,
my flesh is longing for you,
a land parched, weary and waterless. . . .

Your love is better than life itself,
my lips will recite your praise;
all my life I will bless you,
in your name lift up my hands;
my soul will feast most richly,
on my lips a song of joy. . . .

—PSALM 130:1–6; 63:1, 3–5 (JB)

. . . the Spirit
helps us in our weakness;
for we do not know how to pray
as we ought,
but the Spirit himself
intercedes for us
with
sighs too deep for words

—ROMANS 8:26 (RSV)

Heart
reaching
empty and
hungry
hoping

Body
aching
desire
prisoned-in-flesh
roaring

Mind
wondering
wild and
restless
groping

Soul
stretching
strong
a strange joy
soaring

The Bitch-Goddess Success

Blessed are the meek, for they shall inherit the earth

Let me introduce myself. I am a man who at the precocious age of thirty-five experienced an astonishing revelation: it is better to be a success than a failure. Having been penetrated by this great truth concerning the nature of things, my mind was now open for the first time to a series of corollary perceptions, each one as dizzying in its impact as the Original Revelation itself. Money, I now saw (no one, of course, had ever seen it before), was important: it was better to be rich than to be poor. Power, I now saw (moving on to higher subtleties), was desirable: it was better to give orders than to take them. Fame, I now saw (how courageous of me not to flinch), was unqualifiedly delicious: it was better to be recognized than to be anonymous.

This book represents an effort to explain why it should have taken someone like myself so long to arrive at such apparently elementary discoveries. . . .

My second purpose in telling the story of my own career is to provide a concrete setting for a diagnosis of the curiously contradictory feelings our culture instills in us toward the ambition for success, and toward each of its various goals: money, power, fame, and social position. On the one hand, we are commanded to become successful—that is, to acquire more of these worldly goods than we began with, and to do so by our own exertions; on the other hand, it is impressed upon us by means both direct and devious that if we obey the commandment, we shall find ourselves falling victim to the radical corruption of spirit which, given the nature of what is nowadays called the "system," the pursuit of success requires and which its attainment always bespeaks. On the one hand, "the ex-

129

clusive worship of the bitch-goddess SUCCESS," as William James put it in a famous remark, "is our national disease"; on the other hand, a contempt for success is the consensus of the national literature for the past hundred years and more. On the one hand, our culture teaches us to shape our lives in accordance with the hunger for worldly things; on the other hand, it spitefully contrives to make us ashamed of the presence of those hungers in ourselves and to deprive us as far as possible of any pleasure in their satisfaction.

Nothing, I believe, defines the spiritual character of American life more saliently than this contradiction, and I doubt that many Americans, whether they be successes or failures in their careers, can have escaped its consequences. . . .

For taking my career as seriously as I do in this book, I will no doubt be accused of self-inflation and therefore of tastelessness. So be it. There was a time when to talk candidly about sex was similarly regarded as tasteless—a betrayal of what D. H. Lawrence once called "the dirty little secret." For many of us, of course, this is no longer the case. But judging by the embarrassment that a frank discussion of one's feelings about one's own success, or the lack of it, invariably causes in polite company today, ambition (itself a species of lustful hunger) seems to be replacing erotic lust as the prime dirty little secret of the well-educated American soul.

—NORMAN PODHORETZ

So he went in to his father, and said, "My father"; and he said, "Here I am; who are you, my son?" Jacob said to his father, "I am Esau your first-born. I have done as you told me; now sit up and eat of my game, that you may bless me." But Isaac said to his son, "How is it that you have found it so quickly, my son?" He answered, "Because the Lord your God granted me success." Then Isaac said to Jacob, "Come near, that I may feel you, my son, to know whether you really are my son Esau or not." So Jacob went near to Isaac his father, who felt him and said, "The voice is Jacob's voice, but

the hands are the hands of Esau." And he did not recognize
him, because his hands were hairy like his brother Esau's
hands; so he blessed him. He said, "Are you really my son
Esau?" He answered, "I am."

Then he said, "Bring it to me, that I may eat of my son's
game and bless you." So he brought it to him, and he ate;
and he brought him wine, and he drank. Then his father
Isaac said to him, "Come near and kiss me, my son." So he
came near and kissed him; and he smelled the smell of his
garments, and blessed him, and said,

"See, the smell of my son
is as the smell of a field which the Lord has blessed!
May God give you of the dew of heaven,
and of the fatness of the earth,
and plenty of grain and wine.
Let peoples serve you,
and nations bow down to you.
Be lord over your brothers,
and may your mother's sons bow down to you.
Cursed be every one who curses you,
and blessed be every one who blesses you!"

—GENESIS 27:18–29 (RSV)

"Be wise as serpents and innocent as doves."

And James and John, the sons of Zebedee, came forward
to him, and said to him, "Teacher, we want you to do for us
whatever we ask of you." And he said to them, "What do you
want me to do for you?" And they said to him, "Grant us
to sit, one at your right hand and one at your left, in your
glory." But Jesus said to them, "You do not know what you
are asking. Are you able to drink the cup that I drink, or to
be baptized with the baptism with which I am baptized?"
And they said to him, "We are able." And Jesus said to them,
"The cup that I drink you will drink; and with the baptism
with which I am baptized, you will be baptized; but to sit at
my right hand or at my left is not mine to grant, but it is for

those for whom it has been prepared." And when the ten heard it, they began to be indignant at James and John. And Jesus called them to him and said to them, "You know that those who are supposed to rule over the Gentiles lord it over them, and their great men exercise authority over them. But it shall not be so among you; but whoever would be great among you must be your servant." —MARK 10:35–43 (RSV)

How can I be
meek
and still
make it?
a realistic beatitude
would read:
    Blessed are the aggressive
    for they shall reach the top

How can I be
wise
and innocent
together?
I have to choose one
or the other
and it's got to wise:
        smart,
        savvy,
        wary,
        clever
or
I'll get bypassed
passed by
by all those young tigers
breathing on me

I'll admit
I'm in a bind
I'm hungry to make it
I guess
I want power most of all
I, I, I, lots of I's

Lord,
I'm not kidding
I'm not ready to give up
making it
But
could You make me
so real a human being
that making it
would become less desirable
than becoming
myself?

Pearl Is a Treasure

*The kingdom of heaven is like treasure hidden in a field,
which a man found and covered up; then in his joy he
goes and sells all that he has and buys that field. Again,
the kingdom of heaven is like a merchant in search of fine
pearls, who, on finding one pearl of great value, went and
sold all that he had and bought it.*

—MATTHEW 13:44–46 (RSV)

Down in the drugstore off the Warwick Hotel lobby, somebody—in a casual morning throw-on of red slacks, striped
sweater and wrinkled chiffon scarf tied around her hair gypsy-
style—is hunched over a cup of coffee and the theater review
in the *Morning Telegraph*. "They say 'languid eyes' and 'flow-
in' hands.' Honey, I think they're talkin' about a *horse*." The
laughter of the fountain clerks and the cashier's giggles trail
Pearl Bailey past the paperback rack, through the lobby and
up in the elevator to her small high-floor suite for more coffee
and an interview.

"Truly, I'm Dolly. My husband said to me, 'Honey, you
worry too much about people.' I said, 'I don't worry, I *care*.'
Many people worry but they don't do anything about it . . .
I've never understood why people don't recognize what they
have. People see God every day; they just don't recognize Him.

"Look here at this picture of 'The Smiling Christ.' He's always pictured so somber, but when you think about it, the
smiling makes a lot of sense. He prayed, but He didn't pray
all the time. In those days, they laughed, they drank wine,
they talked. Everybody asks me, 'You're religious, aren't you?'
Well, Papa was a reverend, but it isn't really religious at all.
I belong to nothin' except humanity. Every man is religious."

Asked about her reaction to the ecstatic reception for her

"Dolly," she says she has written down how she feels and she brings out a scrap of paper:

"Why do they run? What are they seeking? Love. And with outstretched hands, it's given. The young smile and joke; the old look for hope. Whatever has been given must be shared with all; not relished, but shared. Love is so frighteningly beautiful. Why do they cry? Is it for me or for them? I choose to think it's for 'Deliverance from Despair.' I see their souls, and I hold them gently in my hands and because I love them they weigh nothing. God has set them there so gently I can enjoy their love. Who said people are a burden? They are a delight. My babies, yes they are all my babies, and I shall nurse them with a 'Full Breast of Love.' Take that from me and I shall die. I also feel a great healing power so when they run up to the stage and we touch, I am healed and so are they. The sickness of hate and confusion all disappear and we are all free." —JOAN BARTHEL, *New York Times*

Then Levi had a big feast in his house for Jesus, and there was a large number of tax collectors and other people sitting with them. Some Pharisees and teachers of the Law who belonged to their group complained to Jesus' disciples. "Why do you eat and drink with tax collectors and outcasts?" they asked. Jesus answered them: "People who are well do not need a doctor, but only those who are sick. I have not come to call the respectable people to repent, but the outcasts." Some people said to Jesus, "The disciples of John fast frequently and offer up prayers, and the disciples of the Pharisees do the same; but your disciples eat and drink." Jesus answered: "Do you think you can make the guests at a wedding party go without food as long as the bridegroom is with them? Of course not!. . .

"Now, to what can I compare the people of this day? What are they like? They are like children playing in the marketplace. One group shouts to the other, 'We played wedding music for you, but you would not dance! We sang funeral songs, but you would not cry!' John the Baptist came, and he fasted and drank no wine, and you said, 'He is a madman!' The Son of Man came, and he ate and drank, and you said, 'Look at this man! He is a glutton and wine-drinker, and is a friend of tax collectors and outcasts!' "

—LUKE 5:29–35; 7:31–34 (TEV)

A Pharisee invited Jesus to have dinner with him. Jesus went to his house and sat down to eat. There was a woman in that town who lived a sinful life. She heard that Jesus was eating in the Pharisee's house, so she brought an alabaster jar full of perfume and stood behind Jesus, by his feet, crying and wetting his feet with her tears. Then she dried his feet with her hair, kissed them, and poured the perfume on them. When the Pharisee who had invited Jesus saw this, he said to himself, "If this man were really a prophet, he would know who this woman is who is touching him; he would know what kind of sinful life she leads!" Jesus spoke up and said to him, "Simon, I have something to tell you." "Yes, Teacher," he said, "tell me." "There were two men who owed money to a money-lender," Jesus began; "one owed him five hundred dollars and the other fifty dollars. Neither one could pay him back, so he cancelled the debts of both. Which one, then, will love him more?" "I suppose," answered Simon, "that it would be the one who was forgiven more." "Your answer is correct," said Jesus. Then he turned to the woman and said to Simon: "Do you see this woman? I came into your home, and you gave me no water for my feet, but she has washed my feet with her tears and dried them with her hair. You did not welcome me with a kiss, but she has not stopped kissing my feet since I came. You provided no oil for my head, but she has covered my feet with perfume. I tell you, then, the great love she has shown proves that her many sins have been forgiven. Whoever has been forgiven little, however, shows only a little love."

—LUKE 7:36–47 (TEV)

135

Pearl is a treasure!
thinking of her
makes me smile
she's a kind of Mother Earth
who loves all her children
laughs with us
cries with us
sings and dances with us
she's got hold of
the gospel
and
the gospel's
got hold of her

Pearl is a treasure!
thinking of her
reminds me that
Jesus smiled
laughed
cried
sang and danced
enjoyed parties
with all sorts of human beings
insiders and
outsiders

Pearl is a treasure!
thinking of her
makes me long for
my cup of love
to run over
too
like that woman
who found
forgiveness
was
joy

Pearl is a treasure!
thinking of her
reminds me that
Christianity is not
should not be
    long sermons
        prayers
        meetings
        faces
but joy
like finding
hidden treasure
or
a precious pearl

Faces of the Forgotten

Seek the welfare of the city where I have sent you into exile, and pray to the Lord on its behalf; for in its welfare you will find your welfare.

—JEREMIAH 29:7 (RSV)

Dr. Eric White, the blond, 28-year-old resident who runs the emergency room at night was busy attending to a 52-year-old man who walked into the emergency room at 10:15 P.M., bleeding profusely from a wound.

"We'll take care of you," Dr. White assured him as he led him to a stretcher. "Thank you," replied the man, who was evidently drunk.

After an initial examination, Dr. White who seems to juggle patients as a vaudevillian juggles Indian clubs, summoned two surgical residents who took over the treatment of the stab-wound. . . . Dr. White moved on to a room filled with about 10 persons of assorted ages and ailments, none of them of a critical nature. . . .

Later a man calls to inquire about a neighbor—an elderly woman—who was taken to the emergency room an hour or so earlier in an emaciated and dehydrated condition.

"Has she ever been in a hospital before for any trouble?" Dr. White asks. "We're going to have to go over her and do a few blood tests. No, I can't say exactly what's wrong with her yet."

When he hangs up, Dr. White comments: "Well, that's a help. Usually you don't get anybody calling in like that when a woman lives all alone."

As the pace slackened toward midnight, Dr. White took time to talk to a stooped man of about 60 who had come to the emergency room about 20 times in the last year with assorted complaints.

"What's wrong, Frank?" Dr. White asked.

"I fell twice, and I can't breathe," the man said, putting

down a shopping bag crammed with smaller paper bags, one of which contained dozens of bottles and vials of medication he had collected. "I was weak, Doctor."

"Where are you living now, Frank?"

"The usual place, Grand Central Station. I sit there."

Dr. White listened patiently as the man recounted his ailments, then prescribed a mild analgesic for the pain he complained of. With that, the man picked up his shopping bag and headed back toward Grand Central Terminal.

At midnight, Dr. White briefed his relief, Dr. David-Postlewaite, and Miss Marsalisi took her relief, Mary Rookie, on rounds of the emergency room, and a new shift came on duty.

The corridor was almost deserted by then. The canned music that had played through the evening was no longer heard. Outside the room in which the dehydrated old woman lay, two doctors leaned casually against a stretcher and talked to a visitor.

They pointed out that the city was full of old, lonely people like this woman, who probably had not eaten in days, whose body was covered with the scabs of malnutrition and whose arms bore neat little rows of insect bites.

The woman, they said, should be in a nursing home, but insufficient nursing home facilities make that impossible. Instead, they added, she might remain in Roosevelt for up to five months—costing the city about $5,000 for her care.

"On the other hand," one of the doctors said, "she might be dead in 12 hours."

He paused, then went on.

"How about that," he said. "We stand out here in the hall and talk about how a woman might be dead in 12 hours as if it's nothing. Man, this is really a strange business."

—SYLVAN FOX

While they were there the time came for her to have her child, and she gave birth to a son, her first-born. She

138

wrapped him in swaddling clothes, and laid him in a manger because there was no room for them at the inn.

As they traveled along they met a man on the road who said to him, "I will follow you wherever you go." Jesus answered, "Foxes have holes and the birds of the air have nests, but the Son of Man has nowhere to lay his head."

And at the ninth hour Jesus cried out in a loud voice, "Eloi, Eloi, lama sabachthani!" which means, "My God, my God, why have you deserted me?"
—LUKE 2:6–8; 9:57; MARK 15:34 (JB)

For thus says the Lord God: Behold, I, I myself will search for my sheep, and will seek them out. As a shepherd seeks out his flock when some of his sheep have been scattered abroad, so will I seek out my sheep; and I will rescue them from all places where they have been scattered on a day of clouds and thick darkness. And I will bring them out from the peoples, and gather them from the countries, and will bring them into their own land; and I will feed them on the mountains of Israel, by the fountains, and in all the inhabited places of the country. I will feed them with good pasture, and upon the mountain heights of Israel shall be their pasture; there they shall lie down in good grazing land, and on fat pasture they shall feed on the mountains of Israel. I myself will be the shepherd of my sheep, and I will make them lie down, says the Lord God. I will seek the lost, and I will bring back the strayed, and I will bind up the crippled, and I will strengthen the weak, and the fat and the strong I will watch over; I will feed them in justice.   —EZEKIEL 34:11–16 (RSV)

All the lonely people
where do we all belong?
nowhere
God is nowhere
God is now here

God,
Your heart
must break
when you see
the faces of the forgotten
hidden in the hills
huddled in hotels
and nursing homes
tucked in tenements
stranded in the station
or on the street

Bless all the lonely people
comfort them with kind
relatives, friends, doctors, social workers, policemen
move us
to be willing
to reorder our priorities
to tax ourselves enough
to seek and find
the welfare of the city
where You have sent us

You know
what it's like
to be
rejected
neglected
homeless
hopeless
deserted

That comforts me
Let me comfort
all the lonely people
I know

Be Afraid of Nothing

I am not abandoning you, my children, and I am not betraying you—pay no attention to the slanderous things they will say about me—but this was the way life would have it. Everything is preordained and decided for us by life itself. You must understand that events are taking their inevitable course. Fate has decreed that I leave you, that I change my whole life and not return to that futile existence which I have led for forty years. It is the will of fate, perhaps, that I should do something for the benefit of all—and for you, too, my dear ones.

I have crossed my Rubicon. If you are still there, far away from me, it is so that I may pray for you, so that I may believe with all my heart in our reunion, so that I may be stronger in spirit, so that I may fight and live without despair, so that the pain of it shall cover me like armor. How wise are the ways of Your world, O Lord; You are not giving me this new life just so that I should peacefully enjoy the comforts of the civilized world.

No, Lord, You have given me words I did not know before. You have commanded me to speak the truth to people, to all the people in the world, so that my friends there, in Russia, should also wake from their long sleep, and should be startled out of it, as though by a shot, and come to feel themselves that there can be a limit to what human beings may endure.

It is now early spring, and it is still cold, the leaves are not out yet, but the buds have burst on all the trees and are waiting for warmth.

How fortunate for me that it is almost spring, that I can see round about this eternal and inexorable renewal of life. What a breath of air and how soothing it is, this feeling of expectancy and faith in life, after the death of my husband, after all the indignities which I have endured in Moscow and in Delhi, after all the pain and sorrow, after all the ordeals....

And on sunny days the snow-covered mountains are dazzlingly bright, lakes and rivers glitter, and there is such a ring of triumph all around, from the earth right up to the sky, that the soul wants to leap from the breast and fly up high, singing like a lark, and I am afraid of nothing when my extraordinary world—Your world, O Lord—is so beautiful.

And now it's spring with you too, my children and friends, the snow is melting, the rivers are flowing swiftly. Take a deep breath of the air, which is fermenting like new wine, look up at the sun, and be afraid of nothing, my dear ones, be afraid of nothing.

And do not cry, do not cry, my dear ones—may the spring breathe on you with its fresh breezes and help you to believe in the inevitable victory and rebirth of life.

—SVETLANA ALLILUYEVA

Another to whom he said, "Follow me," replied, "Let me go and bury my father first." But he answered, "Leave the dead to bury their dead; your duty is to go and spread the news of the kingdom of God."

Another said, "I will follow you, sir, but first let me go and say goodbye to my people at home." Jesus said to him, "Once the hand is laid on the plough, no one who looks back is fit for the kingdom of God."   —LUKE 9:59–62 (JB)

When he had finished speaking he said to Simon, "Put out into deep water and pay out your nets for a catch." "Master," Simon replied, "we worked hard all night long and caught nothing, but if you say so, I will pay out the nets." And when they had done this they netted such a huge number of fish that their nets began to tear, so they signalled to their com-

panions in the other boat to come and help them; when these
came, they filled the two boats to sinking point.

When Simon Peter saw this he fell at the knees of Jesus
saying, "Leave me, Lord; I am a sinful man." For he and all
his companions were completely overcome by the catch they
had made . . . But Jesus said to Simon, "Do not be afraid;
from now on it is men you will catch." Then, bringing their
boats back to land, they left everything and followed him.

—LUKE 5:1–11 (JB)

But now, thus says Yahweh,
who created you, Jacob,
who formed you, Israel:
    Do not be afraid, for I have redeemed you;
    I have called you by your name, you are mine.
    Should you pass through the sea, I will be with you;
    or through rivers, they will not swallow you up.
    Should you walk through fire, you will not be scorched
    and the flames will not burn you.
    For I am Yahweh, your God,
    the Holy One of Israel, your saviour.

I will bring your offspring from the east,
and gather you from the west.
To the north I will say, "Give them up"
and to the south, "Do not hold them."
Bring back my sons from far away,
my daughters from the end of the earth,
all those who bear my name,
whom I have created for my glory,
whom I have formed, whom I have made.

—ISAIAH 43:1–7 (JB)

143

Have I crossed my Rubicon?
a border is frightening
back is home
beyond is homeless
security is behind
uncertainty is ahead
　　look forward,
　　　　　　then
　　　　　　now

Have I crossed my Rubicon?
I'm afraid
to risk everything
for the unknown
courage
costs more than
caution
but promises more

Have I crossed my Rubicon?
new life
is threat
as well as
promise
end
as well as
beginning

Have I crossed my Rubicon?
faith
is stronger than
fear
my time is coming
the time to cross
not without
fear

　　look forward,
　　　　　　then
　　　　　　now

70 71 72 73 10 9 8 7 6 5 4 3

144